Reserve Bank of India

cTom

Indian Independent Thinkers (IIT)
Think Tank

Copyright © 2016

ISBN:

ISBN-13: 978-1537776019
ISBN-10:   1537776010

CONTENTS

-- FOREWORD	4
-- PREFACE	5
-- Introduction	7
1. Evolution of Modern Banking	7
2 Slide of Rupee	14
3 Compromised Universities	15
4 Colonial India	18
5 Bank of International Settlements (BIS).	24
6 Evil Twins: IMF and WB	31
7 World Currency	41
8 Experts recommend New World Currency	46
9 Money and Banking in USA	49
10 Federal Reserve Bank	57
11 Rothchilds	69
12 The Curse of Central Banks	92
13 The Three World Wars	98
14 Recap and Conclusion	100
-- Other Books by Same Author	107
-- About the Author	108
-- Acknowledgements.	108
-- Legal Disclaimers	108

FOREWORD

'Reserve Bank of India' is a light hearted look at India's central bank and its history. It is written in simple non-technical fictional style language anybody can understand. India's central bank is a link in the chain of central banks that binds and holds together the economies of the whole world. Most Indians and even members of the governing board of RBI are unaware how RBI works. What is Rajan doing in Switzerland every week? What causes inflation? Where is Rupee headed? What currency will Indians use in the very near future? Who controls finances of every Indian citizen? Who is conspiring to destroy India and why? This book explains everything in simple everyman's language. Once I opened the book, I could not put it down until I finished it. I learned a lot of things which I never knew until now. I recommend this book to my Professors.

Dr. Kenneth Moore

PREFACE

The fathers of US Constitution came from Europe and they have seen the destruction and devastation caused by central banks in Europe. They wisely gave treasury and only treasury the authority to mint money. They did not want a central bank in USA.

There is a saying that 'money is the root of all evil'. Actually, 'interest on money is the root of all evil'. The destructive power of usury was understood even in ancient times. Moses prohibited usury among Jews, but encouraged Jews to lend on interest to non-Jews, as a means to destroying and enslaving the societies of non-Jews. Jesus cursed and drove out the money-changers (bankers) from the Temple. Christianity frowned upon usury. Prophet Mohammed banned usury and called it the devil.

Jews took the advice of Moses and practiced usury among European Christians. Rothschild established central banks in Europe. Central banks were a cleverly disguised usury pyramid scheme. Through creating and financing wars in Europe, Rothschild grew very wealthy and powerful. The Talmud, a vulgar interpretation of Jewish Scriptures, says Jews are entitled to rule the world. Rothschild decided to make this a reality and laid out plans to enslave the whole world through the use of usury and create 'one world government' to be ruled by Rothschild'.

Rothschild established central banks in every country. By creating money out of thin air and then charging interest on it, central banks put the countries under the yoke of debt. By increasing and then decreasing the money supply, the central banks create inflation and deflation, prosperity and economic depressions in their countries. They wove intricate economic spider-web around the governments of the world to keep them within the Rothschild debt choke hold. The future is a 'one-world currency' and 'one world government' under the control of Rothschild.

This book is an interesting and informative read. I have worked in banking and in economics for 40 years. I never knew that Rothschild family was behind all the wars and revolutions and depressions and inflations in this world. I had no idea that Reserve Bank of India is a Rothchild bank. After reading this book, I realized that the whole world is moving towards a one world government to be ruled by Rothschild. One of the goals of the one world government is to reduce population to 500 million. I shudder at the thought that my children and my grandchildren would be culled to make Rothschild's NWO a reality. This book opened my eyes to the evil of central banks.

Dr. J Cryan

Reserve Bank of India

Introduction

During my world travels, I have come across owners of large financial enterprises, Professors of Economics in Prestigious Universities, Finance ministers of countries, Governors of Central Banks and numerous PhDs from Prestigious universities, who did not know that FED is a private bank or how FED was set up or why Central banks have to obey orders of BIS. I wrote this book to educate those who want to know. When you know how the system works, you will understand why all the economics theories and formulas (even Nobel Prize winning ones) cannot predict the future course of economy. This book is dedicated to Professor Surajit Sinha of IIT Kanpur, India. An email from him prompted me to write this book.

1. Evolution of Modern Banking

Modern Banking system started out in mediaeval Europe where society was in constant turmoil due to constant widespread robbery, murder, kidnapping, conflicts and wars. Gold was the wealth. People needed a place to keep it safe. Khazari Jews who settled in Europe lived in their own enclaves. They spoke their own strange language which outsiders did not understand and they were protected by their own armed thugs and gangs. Jewish goldsmiths who operated inside these Jewish enclaves offered to safekeep gold. People took advantage of this service and deposited their gold with these goldsmiths for safekeeping. The goldsmiths would give a receipt for the deposit of gold with them. People used to trade the receipts of deposits in place of gold because it was more convenient than carrying gold around. Whenever somebody needed the gold, they could go to the goldsmiths and surrender the receipt and get their gold. In India, even today, people pawn their gold with pawn shops and take out loans. The pawnshops will wrap up the gold Jewelry and keep it in their safe and give a receipt. When the loan amount is returned with interest and the receipt surrendered, the package of gold jewelry will be returned to customer. If the customer die or lose the receipt, he will not be able to redeem his gold.

The actual gold could sit in the safe box for long time while the deposit-receipts kept changing hands in business. This is the beginning of bank notes or exchangeable gold based currency. The currency was issued by the goldsmith, a private entity. The gold deposits were like the gold reserve and receipts of deposit were like the reserve currency or currency based on reserves. It was an exchangeable currency which means one could exchange it for the gold at any time.

When the receipt is exchanged for gold, the goldsmith will charge a fee for safekeeping. The longer the gold was in safekeeping, the higher the fee. This is the interest the goldsmith charged. Thus the deposit-receipts were interest-bearing. The deposit-receipts were issued as currency in business transactions. It was an interest-bearing currency. The value of the currency steadily decreased by the amount of the interest that it accumulated. For example, if the depositor kept 100 grams of gold with the goldsmith, and got a receipt for the deposit, and he traded it for 100 goats, and the got merchant came and surrendered the receipt, the goldsmith may give back the 100 grams of gold minus 6 grams for his fee for keeping the gold or interest on the receipt (currency). The receipt for 100 grams of gold will only get back 94 grams of gold after one year. In this case, the receipt (currency) has an inflation rate of 6%.

Safekeeping gold and issuing receipt came to be known as banking. When the receipts were used in trade in place of gold, the receipts became currency (money). When goldsmiths (now bankers) started charging a fee for safekeeping of gold, the receipts became interest bearing currency. The fee for safekeeping when expressed as a percentage of the gold on deposit, it became the rate of inflation. Thus, the receipts of gold deposits became an interest bearing (inflation based) currency. These receipts were issued by goldsmiths, which were private businesses, in their banking activity. Receipts from different goldsmiths were compatible because they were based on gold deposited with goldsmiths. The goldsmiths were predominantly Jews. Similar to Gujarathis dominating the Gold and diamond Jewelry business in India.

Jews in goldsmith business were very ruthless, cunning, conniving fraudsters and gangsters. When somebody brings in a large amount of gold for deposit, the goldsmith may tip off the gangsters. That customer may be attacked or killed and robbed of his deposit receipt, on the way home or later at home. Same way, if a depositor withdraws a large amount of gold, the goldsmith may tip off his gangsters. That customer may be attacked and robbed or killed on his way back or in his house. The goldsmiths themselves will appear to conduct business honestly; otherwise they will be driven out of the community. But anonymous gangsters can deprive people of their gold. When the news of gangsters and robbery spread, people got scared and they deposited all their gold with goldsmiths for safekeeping.

In the course of time, goldsmiths noticed that only a small fraction of their customers came back for their gold at any time. They started lending some of the gold which they were safekeeping, to others for a fee or interest. As long as the customer brought back the gold before it was demanded by the depositor, the depositor would not know any difference.

The borrowers of gold themselves could deposit the gold with the goldsmiths and get a receipt which was more convenient than carrying gold around. Thus depositor A could have a receipt for 100 grams of gold deposited with goldsmith X. Then customer B could take a loan of that same 100 grams of gold and pay a fee or interest. Customer B may decide to take a receipt for 100 grams of gold instead, because it was more convenient than carrying gold around. Now there are two receipts for 100 grams of gold in circulation based on the same 100 grams of physical gold. The Goldsmith would earn interest or fee twice for safekeeping 100 grams of gold. Goldsmiths found out that this was very profitable business.

The amount shown in receipts is 2 x 100 = 200 grams of gold. The actual amount of gold in safekeeping is only 100 grams of gold. Or, in other words, the gold in safekeeping or reserve is only a fraction of the amount in receipts in circulation, in this case ½ or 50%. Each receipt has only a fraction of its value in reserve, in this case 50%. This system of giving out receipts or currency based on only a fraction of it in reserve is called fractional reserve banking.

Only one of the depositors might show up and demand his gold back, at any one time. If he takes out the gold, he will be satisfied that his gold was safe with the goldsmith and he will happily redeposit the gold with the same now-trusted-goldsmith and get a fresh receipt and use it in place of actual gold. If, by chance, both depositors A and B show up and demand their gold, the goldsmith will not be able to return their gold in full. When most of the customers show up and demand their gold at the same time, it will be called a 'run on the bank'. Goldsmith may close his business and declare bankruptcy. Jews have always been crooks. A goldsmith could take in all the gold as deposits and then secretly leave the country with all the gold and in that situation the customers would be out of luck. A goldsmith could stage an attack and robbery by gangsters and claim that all his gold was stolen and hence he cannot restore the deposits. Deceit and fraud was the hallmark of Jewish bankers.

After depositing 100 grams of gold with goldsmith X, depositor A receives a receipt for 100 grams. He can buy 100 goats for 100 gram of gold. But, if A wants only 50 goats, then he will have to go back to goldsmith X and ask for two receipts for 50 grams of gold each. So, to make life easy for depositor A, goldsmith X may issue 100 receipts, each for 1 gram of gold. If Goldsmith X decides to standardize his receipts, he may issue 1 gram denominated receipts for his deposits. Such receipts would be called a standard currency (bank notes) with face value of 1 gram of gold, or, X's 1 gram banknotes, which anybody can take to the goldsmith X (Bank X) and get 1 gram of gold minus a safekeeping fee.

People deposited their gold with X and got receipt or 1 gram denominated receipts or bank notes, for convenience. So, they would not want to get their gold back and be inconvenienced again. So, the bank notes may continue to circulate in the community as means of business and gold will remain with goldsmith X as reserve.

Let us assume the price of goats is 1 gram of gold for 1 goat. This price does not change. Goats are in demand, and the goat farmers could always get 100 grams of gold for 100 goats. But, if the farmer accepts X's bank notes for 100 grams, he can exchange it for only 100 grams minus safekeeping fee from X. The bank fees will erode away the amount of gold redeemable with these bank notes. If the safekeeping fee or inflation is 6% per year, after one year, the bank note for 100 grams will be redeemable for only 94 grams. The merchant who bought 100 goats for 100 grams would have to sell them after one year for bank notes for 106 grams to break even. The buyer could buy 100 goats for banknotes for 100 grams last year, but this year he has to pay bank notes for 106 grams for the same goats. The merchant receives only 100 grams for his 100 goats even though the buyer spent bank notes for 106 grams. This is called price inflation when using bank notes from X. The difference between actual price (100 grams) and the price one has to pay (106 grams) goes into the pocket of X as his fee or profit.

After using X's banknotes for a while, people forgot that they had no inflation when they were using gold for commercial transactions. They came to believe that inflation is natural and it is somehow their fault. May be they did not bargain harder or because there was less production or natural calamities or increased demand or something of that sort. They will never blame X for causing this inflation. In fact, X may come out as a savior of the economy, by reducing the interest he charges on the bank notes. When the interest is reduced, the inflation will be reduced. People will praise X as the savior of economy.

Jews are scrupulous manipulators of this world. They will periodically reduce the amount of receipts (bank notes) they issue and that will mean there will be fewer bank notes available to do business transactions. When people cannot transact business for lack of currency, the businesses will lay off employees. Unemployment will increase poverty. When people are unemployed, there will be less demand for goods. That will lead to more layoffs and businesses may close. When people have no money they will default on loans and lose their houses and properties to creditors. People will start selling their property for less. Property values will plummet. This is called an economic depression. At that time, Jews will come in with a lot of X's bank notes and buy up all the property and businesses at low prices. Then X will start issuing more bank notes. Then prosperity will increase. The Jews who bought all that property at rock bottom prices can now sell it for high prices and make huge profits or simply keep the property and businesses for themselves. This is called a boom and bust cycle. By causing such boom and bust cycles, Jews have already acquired all the businesses and property in this world.

X will not allow anybody to audit his business. People simply have to assume that he has enough gold in reserve to pay off all the bank notes that are in circulation. Each bank note is a promise to exchange the bank note for gold on demand. But for an ordinary banknote holder, demanding exchange to gold will be a problem. When faced with a problem, goldsmith X may call in his thugs to take care of the poor depositor.

"History records that the money changers [bankers] have used every form of abuse, intrigue, deceit, and violent means possible to maintain their control over governments by controlling money and its issuance." - President James Madison

2 Slide of Rupee

India is an overpopulated poor country. People spend all their lives scrounging for food and shelter and basic necessities of life. They trust their Gods to bring them good fortune and they trust their government to bring them prosperity. They do not want to know more about or to think much about their Gods or their government. Their trusted gods have blessed them with too many children and the land cannot produce enough food to keep them alive. Their trusted governments have brought them the illusion of wealth but their buying power steadily decreases through inflation. The more money they get in their hands the less purchasing power they have. Everything is going up in price except their meager income which does not keep up with inflation.

Long time ago Lord Krishna promised that whenever 'adharma' (evil) increase beyond limit, Vishnu (God) 'sambhavami yuge yuge' (will arrive periodically) to destroy the evil and establish balance of good and evil on this earth. But, instead of Lord Krishna, all we see is new governors of RBI. They all have PhD from America and they all have the same goal: to rob India and make it poor and subservient to foreign powers. It appears as though they all work for foreign powers and they all follow the same path. Are they really agents of enemies of India or are they simply misguided in their thinking? Did their education in America make them like that? Or, were they recruited by foreign powers while they were studying abroad? All these are possibilities. Manmohan Singh, Duvvuri Subbarao and Rajan all wreaked havoc with Indian economy and devalued the currency to $1 = Rs.66. India is going in the footsteps of Zimbabwe. In 2015, US$1 = 35 quadrillion Zimbabwean currency.

.
.
.
.
.

3. Compromised Universities

Is it possible that those who fill the positions in RBI and economic advisory committee of PM were misled or bought by enemies of the country while they were educated in USA? Universities are supposed to be places of pure unbiased learning. However, in America, Universities have been compromised. In 1971, future Supreme court Justice Lewis Powell wrote a memorandum to Eugene Snydor of the US Chamber of Commerce. Later, this came to be known as the Powell Manifesto. In it, Powell suggested that the legislature has passed several anti-business laws and that American businesses should use their power and money to fight back. He wrote: "American economic system is under broad attack... Business must learn the lesson . . . that political power is necessary; that such power must be assiduously cultivated; and that when necessary, it must be used aggressively and with determination—without embarrassment and without the reluctance which has been so characteristic of American business.... Strength lies in organization, in careful long-range planning and implementation, in consistency of action over an indefinite period of years, in the scale of financing available only through joint effort, and in the political power available only through united action and national organizations."

One of the actions they took was to get like-minded faculty hired at universities and produce propaganda textbooks for use in the universities and produce research papers favorable to their cause. Or, in other words, the corporations turned universities into brainwashing centers for future intelligencia. In addition, foreign students were prime targets for CIA recruiting on campuses. These foreign students go back with prestigious degrees and enter into powerful positions in their home countries. From their positions, they will do the dirty work of CIA and of the subversive banking houses like IMF, World Bank and BIS.

The Koch brothers and other wealthy businessmen poured money into conservative media and politics. Businessmen work on all sides of the issue. Those ultra-rightwing activists who call themselves neo-liberals worked on the Republican Party side and also on the Democratic Party side and influenced politics and media. Numerous 'think tanks' and study centers were established to propagandize for them.

Selective hiring of faculty for purposes of brainwashing students continues even today in universities. Recently news reports surfaced that Koch Brothers sought power to control academic hiring in return for donations to universities. In Florida State University, they sought appointment of ultra-rightwing economics faculty in return for a grant. They did same in and provided grants to 162 other universities and colleges across the country in 2012 alone. Their memo said: "As we all know, there are no free lunches. Everything comes with costs. In this case, the money for faculty lines and graduate students is coming from a group of funding organizations with strong libertarian views. These organizations have an explicit agenda. "They want to expose students to what they believe are vital concepts about the benefits of the market and the dangers of government failure, and they want to support and mentor students who share their views. Therefore, they are trying to convince us to hire faculty who will provide exposure and mentoring. If we are not willing to hire such faculty, they are not willing to fund us."

The documents date back to 2007, when the Koch deal was first being negotiated with FSU. Among the other demands made by the foundation was that Benson, a free-market libertarian who shares many of the Kochs' beliefs, must have his term as chair of the economics department extended for three years as a requirement of the donation.

Reporter Dave Levinthal: "The documents give a blueprint of what the Kochs wanted and if ultimately they didn't get everything they demanded it still gives a rare view into their intentions. They were saying 'we want this, this and that, and if you don't do it, we are not going to give you any money'."

Every Indian citizen is affected by money and its shrinking value and therefore every Indian citizen should ask the question: is RBI working for the country or for foreign powers? The workings of RBI are a mystery even to the board of directors of RBI. How does it function? How is it set up? Who controls it? Even though truthful information about RBI is unavailable, we can learn a lot about it by studying BoE because RBI was setup by BoE in its own image.

4. Colonial India

In the ancient times, People used cows and other cattle as wealth. Ancient Vedic scriptures talk about coins called 'rupa'. 'Arthashastra', written by Chanakya, prime minister to the first Maurya emperor Chandragupta Maurya (340–290 BC), mentions Suvarna-rupa (gold coins), rupya-rupa (silver coins), Tamara-rupa (copper coins) and Sisa-rupa (lead coins). Rupa means form or image. In 1540 AD, Mughal emperor Sher Shah Suri issued a standardized coin of silver, weighing 178 grains, called "Rupiya". These silver coins remained in use through the British rule of India.

Chinese used leather notes from 1st century BC and paper notes from 7th century AD. British banks started using paper currency in India in 18th century.

The name 'India' was given to their colony by British East India Company. They minted their own coins in gold and business was transacted using weight of gold. Then Bank of England (BoE) took over management of 'currency and credit' in India. Following WWI, Hilton Young commission was appointed to make a proposal to set up a central bank for India. Dr. B. R. Ambedkar had written a book "The Problem of the Rupee – Its origin and its solution" in 1923. When Hilton Young Commission came to India, each and every member were holding Dr. Ambedkar's book. RBI was conceptualized as per the guidelines, working style and outlook presented by Dr. Ambedkar in front of the Hilton Young Commission. The legislative assembly passed those recommendations as 'RBI act 1934'. As per the legislation, RBI was established on April 1st, 1935, '..to regulate the issue of Bank Notes and keeping of reserves with a view to securing monetary stability in India and generally to operate the currency and credit system of the country to its advantage.' BoE set up the RBI as a private bank, with BoE as the sole shareholder, and it would keep a fractional reserve of Gold and Silver and then mint money against it and lend to the Government of India at 7% interest and extend credit to other banks.

Ambedkar was taught by his British masters that everything British was ideal and BoE was the perfect central bank. He never knew that BoE was a private bank, independent of any sort of Government controls or oversight. He never understood the evils of private central banks. Even if he had, the outcome would have been same. If he had envisioned anything different from BoE model, he would have been considered a crazy nut. Even in 21st century, opponents and critiques of central banks, like Dr. Ron Paul in USA, are considered crazy nuts and influential nuts are suicided. (suicided = murdering someone and then reporting it as suicide).

The name 'Reserve Bank' implied that the bank had some reserve of Gold to issue coins for India. 'Of India' implied that this bank was owned by the government of India. The bank took in all the gold and silver of the country and used it as fractional reserve against which Indian coins – Rupees – were issued. RBI kept the gold and silver reserves in BoE's secret underground vaults in England. Indian money consisted of copper coins and paper currencies. The money minted by RBI was loaned to the government at 7% interest. The Government then spent the money for various government expenses like salary for its employees and the army and for various government projects. The government was supposed to pay the principal and interest back to the RBI in gold and silver.

The country was divided into administrative districts and a tax collector was appointed for each district. They functioned as local administrators also. They were called collectors. That name holds to this day. The taxes collected by collectors were sent to the treasury under armed escort. The treasury paid the principal and interest on the money that was loaned to the government. When the treasury fell short, it borrowed more money from RBI to cover the deficit.

Let us say the government borrowed 100 rupees from RBI and spent it for salaries of soldiers and bureaucrats. The soldiers and bureaucrats spent that money for food and clothing and shelter and other necessities. The businesses that provided food and clothing and shelter spent that money to acquire more goods and services. Thus the 100 rupees circulated in the country for one year. At end of year the treasury has collected, let us say, 50 rupees as taxes and penalties and fees from the people and the army has conquered another small Indian kingdom and plundered it and got 200 rupees worth of gold and silver. The treasury has to pay to RBI, the principal 100 rupees and 7% interest (total 107 rupees) in gold and silver. The price of gold and silver was fixed in rupees permanently. So, it does not matter if the price of gold and silver increased or decreased in the market, the treasury will pay back the rupees in gold at the fixed exchange rate. Next year the process will repeat all over again.

The RBI will keep the gold and silver worth 107 rupees as reserve and make more paper and copper money and lend to the government as needed. Let us say that the government borrowed 100 rupees. The war that year was more costly than expected or the plunder was less than usual. The money that was collected as taxes and the plunder from the conquered Indian kingdom together came to be about 90 rupees worth of gold and silver. In that case the treasury will pay to RBI 90 rupees worth of gold and silver and owe 17 rupees. The treasury cannot borrow 17 rupees from RBI and pay off the debt because the RBI will accept only gold and silver, not paper and copper. Next year, let us say, the government borrow 100 rupees in copper and paper money from RBI. At end of year, it will have to pay back 100 in principal and 17 in unpaid bill from previous year (total principal = Rs. 117) and interest on Rs. 117 at 7%, in gold and silver. The deficits can accumulate over the years and become very substantial portion of the GDP. In 2015, American government owed over 15 trillion dollars to its central bank.

The system worked well because India had accumulated a lot of gold and silver over thousands of years and the British army could just go and plunder it from palaces of local Indian kings and from temples. India's temple treasures made England and owners of BoE rich. The Padmanabhaswamy Temple, in Trivandrum, in the Indian state of Kerala, escaped the notice of the British. In 2012, 8 secret vaults of treasurers worth over a trillion dollars, accumulated over 2400 years, were found and opened by Government of India. Indian Supreme court removed the Trivandrum Royal Family from temple administration after hundreds of years in that position and confiscated the treasure and put government operatives in charge. Naturally a lot of the treasure was pilfered.

Government could not always come up with enough gold and silver to repay RBI. So the money owed to RBI steadily grew. Over the years, India was flooded with copper and paper money and all the gold and silver from the country stacked up in secret vaults of BoE in England.

RBI loaned money to other banks in the country also. While the interest rate for the loans to the government remained the same at 7%, the RBI charged other banks as much interest as they could. That was called the interbank loan rate and it changed periodically.

When India got freedom from British rule, RBI became central bank of 'free India'. When the Britishers left, RBI had a bundle of paper currency and a bag of copper coins in its vaults. There was no record or accounting of how much gold and silver was shipped to BoE. Repayment of the huge debt, accumulated over years, owed to RBI by British Indian government became the responsibility of the new 'free India'.

Later, on the basis of the Reserve Bank of India (Transfer to Public Ownership) Act, 1948, RBI was nationalized with effect from 1st January, 1949. All shares in the capital of the Bank were deemed transferred to the Central Government on payment of a suitable compensation. However, the government of India could not pay off all the money that was owed to RBI in gold and silver. So, that amount was converted to shares in the new RBI. The RBI continues to mint and lend money to Government of India for interest. The shareholders of RBI, which now includes Government of India, receive share of the profits from interest every year.

In August 2015, RBI paid a dividend of nearly Rs 66,000 crore ($10 billion) to the government, the highest ever from the central bank in its 80-year history. It was 22% more than it paid in 2014. Newspapers reported: ".. this payment can help ease the government's finances, help meet its fiscal deficit targets, provide liquidity to the system so that the rate of interest remains low and also make available funds for the government's capital expenditure. RBI's payment was seen as another proof of its active support to the government's initiatives to kick start the slowing economy..." The average educated reader never asks the question, how is RBI helping India, if it first takes 25 billion from India and then returns 10 billion of that back to India.

If RBI was truly nationalized and if RBI is truly working for the people and of the people and by the people, it would not be printing paper and loaning it to the government and charging interest. It is India's money; India does not have to borrow its own money from a mostly-foreign-owned for-profit corporation and pay interest. Nehru and Indira Gandhi were both aware of the evil in RBI but they were unable to do anything about it. If India discontinue RBI and start printing its own money, there will be severe consequences. If Government of India had nationalized RBI without compensation to its shareholder, there would have been severe consequences as well. For example: (1) India could have been blacklisted and blocked from using International Bank of Settlements (BIS). BIS can literally wipe any country out of the map of the world. What? USSR with its nuclear arsenal can be wiped out of the map of the world by BIS? Yes, BIS can wipe out any

country from the map of the world.
(2) SWIFT may disconnect India from its network and foreign banks may refuse to handle any transactions of India.
(3) The financial assets of India that are located overseas may be confiscated or frozen.
(4) Foreign agents may start civil unrest and political turmoil in India and replace and even kill the political leaders who nationalized RBI.
(5) Foreign countries could militarily attack India and destabilize or conquer and colonize India or completely wipe out India from the map of the world.

Countries survived without BIS until 1930. They can continue to survive for ever without BIS, can't they? Haven't North Korea, Libya, Syria, Iran, Iraq and Cuba survived all these years without having any associations with BIS? Why don't the politicians and central bankers think about that?

5 Bank of International Settlements (BIS)

BIS was founded by BoE and its daughter Banks, in Basel, Switzerland, in 1930. It has been called "the most secretive and most powerful evil organization in the world." Its headquarters was in Hotel Savoy-Univers. The BIS was established after WWI to handle reparation payments of Germany to other countries. It is a private Bank. BoE is its major shareholder. Only central banks that are approved by BIS are allowed to open accounts in BIS. Being a private bank, BIS can decide who will be allowed to open an account in it and who will be allowed to transact business through it. It has been observed that BIS does business with only central banks which are partially or fully owned by BoE. As of now, North Korea, Iran, Syria, and Cuba are the only countries that do not have a BoE owned central bank and naturally these countries do not have accounts in BIS.

Having an account at the BIS is very crucial to the survival of a country. It handles transactions between central banks. For example, when India exports some goods to 'country A', unless there is some barter agreements between India and 'country A', India will receive payments in 'currency A'. India may save 'Currency A' payments in its account at BIS or convert it into another currency at BIS. Similarly when India imports some goods from 'Country B', it will be paid in Indian currency, which has no usefulness for 'country B'. The 'country B' will receive payment in a useful currency through BIS. Without mediation of BIS, international trade is difficult.

Professor Carroll Quigley of Georgetown University studied BIS for 20 years and then wrote: " the international bankers would control and manipulate the money system of a nation while letting it appear to be controlled by the government.....[BIS] had another far-reaching aim, ... to create a world system of financial control in private hands able to dominate the political system of each country and the economy of the world as a whole. This system was to be controlled in a feudalist fashion by the central banks of the world acting in concert, by secret agreements arrived at in frequent private meetings and conferences. The apex of the system was to be BIS in Basel, Switzerland, a private bank owned and controlled by the world's central banks which were themselves private corporations owned by Rothschild family."

In 1791, Mayer Amschel Bauer Rothschild said: "Allow me to issue and control a nation's currency, and I care not who makes its laws." His five sons established private central banks in London, Paris, Vienna, Berlin and Naples. These banks were outside the control of the governments. Later they established private central banks in every country. Central banks print money. The governments must borrow this money to run their business. The result is a global economy in which not only industry but government itself runs on "credit" (or debt) created by private banks. Duvvuri and Rajan, when they were chairmen of RBI, used to attend secret meetings at BIS and take instructions from them and used to subvert Indian economy. They also demanded that they (RBI) should be independent from the control of Government of India. BIS insists that the economic and political systems of nations must be controlled by bankers, for the benefit of bankers, not by citizens for the country's benefit.

BIS has governmental immunity, pays no taxes, and has its own private police force and it is above the law in all respects. Its shareholders and employees have their own BIS passports and full diplomatic immunity. Its operations are done in complete secrecy. It has several concentric circles of power and decision making. Those who are in the outer circles do not know who are in the inner circles. The outermost circle consists of over 100 central banks. The inner circle is believed to consist of 55 or so key central banks. The circle within the inner circle is believed to have about 15 to 18 members. People in the outer circles do not know who is part of the inner circle. There are several circles within this inner of the inner circle also. No information is available about the innermost circle and who is part of it or how it operates. It is a mystery how Rothschild communicates with the innermost circle. It has even been speculated that perhaps Rothschild is the innermost circle. Each circle implements the decisions taken by the circle inside of it. These secret circles are set up in the fashion of the Freemasons society.

"The prime value, which also seems to demarcate the inner club from the rest of the BIS members, is the firm belief that central banks should act independently of their home governments. . . . A second and closely related belief of the inner club is that politicians should not be trusted to decide the fate of the international monetary system."

In 1974, BIS created the 'Basel Committee on Banking Supervision'. Besel is the city in Switzerland where BIS is located. Incidentally, WWI and WWII affected all the countries of Europe except Switzerland. That is because the International bankers who financed and directed these wars were located there. The members of this committee were chosen by BIS. The Committee, in turn, sets the rules, including capital requirements and reserve controls, for banking globally

Joan Veon: "The BIS is where all of the world's central banks meet to analyze the global economy and determine what course of action they will take next, to put more money in their pockets, since they control the amount of money in circulation and how much interest they are going to charge governments and banks for borrowing from them. . . . When you understand that the BIS pulls the strings of the world's monetary system, then you understand that they have the ability to create a financial boom or bust in a country. If that country is not doing what the money lenders want, then all they have to do is sell its currency."

In 1988, Japan was doing very well and it was the biggest creditor in the world. BIS decided to destroy the economy of Japan, the most robust economy in the world at the time. BIS issued a memo requiring all banks to raise their bank capital from 6 to 8%. Raising the capital requirement forced the Japanese banks to cut back on lending, creating a major recession in Japan. Property prices fell and loans were defaulted as the security for them shriveled up. This set in motion a downward spiral and the banks went bankrupt. The banks were taken over by government.

India was also affected. The BIS capital adequacy standards required loans to private borrowers to be "risk-weighted," with the degree of risk determined by private rating agencies. Farmers and small business owners could not afford the agencies' fees. Banks therefore assigned 100 percent risk to the loans, and then resisted extending credit to these "high-risk" borrowers because more capital was required to cover the loans. Hundreds of Indian farmers, unable to get loans, committed suicide. The Indian government was sympathetic to the plight of farmers but it was unable to help them for fear of offending the BIS.

In 2008, Korean entrepreneurs with good collateral couldn't get operational loans from Korean banks, at a time when the economic downturn required increased investment and easier credit. 'The Bank of Korea has provided more than 35 trillion won to banks since September of that year when the global financial crisis reached its peak. But the banks did not lend it out and they kept the money in order to satisfy the requirements of BIS. That led to many bankruptcies.'

Professor Chang Ha-joon, of Cambridge University: 'What banks do for their own interests, or to improve the BIS ratio, is against the interests of the whole society. This is a bad idea.' BIS can force national banking systems in a way contrary to the developmental needs of their national economies. Economist Henry C K Liu: "National banking systems are suddenly thrown into the rigid arms of the Basel Capital Accord sponsored by the Bank of International Settlement (BIS), or to face the penalty of usurious risk premium in securing international interbank loans. . . . National policies suddenly are subjected to profit incentives of private financial institutions, all members of a hierarchical system controlled and directed from the money center banks in New York. The result is to force national banking systems to privatize . . . BIS regulations serve only the single purpose of strengthening the international private banking system, even at the peril of national economies. . . . The IMF and the international banks regulated by the BIS are a team: the international banks lend recklessly to borrowers in emerging economies to create a foreign currency debt crisis; the IMF arrives as a carrier of monetary virus in the name of sound monetary policy; then the international banks come as vulture investors in the name of financial rescue to acquire national banks deemed capital-inadequate and insolvent by the BIS... Ironically, developing countries with their own natural resources did not actually need the foreign investment that trapped them in debt to outsiders. Applying the State Theory of Money, which assumes that a sovereign nation has the power to issue its own money, any government can fund with its own currency all its domestic developmental needs to maintain full employment without inflation.... When governments fall into the trap of accepting loans in foreign currencies, however, they become "debtor nations" subject to IMF and BIS regulation. They are forced to divert their production to exports, just to earn the foreign currency necessary to pay the interest on their loans. National banks deemed "capital inadequate" have to deal with strictures comparable to the "conditionalities" imposed by the IMF on debtor nations: "escalating capital requirement, loan write-offs and liquidation, and restructuring through selloffs, layoffs, downsizing, cost-cutting and freeze on capital spending... Reversing the logic that a sound banking system should lead to full employment and developmental growth, BIS regulations demand high unemployment and developmental degradation in national economies as the fair price for a sound global private banking system."

The developing economies were devastated one by one. The large banks in USA however avoided the Basel rules by separating the "risk" of default out from the loans and selling it off to investors, using a form of derivative known as "credit default swaps." They bundled together all the risky loans and sold it to investors. When the housing bubble burst, the risky loans were defaulted and the American economy went into recession.

Thus BIS can cause great economic turmoil in any country. What will happen if the banks do not follow the orders of BIS? North Korea, Cuba, Iran, Syria and Libya were not affected by BIS orders and they survived unscathed. Other countries also would be unscathed if their banks simply ignored BIS and its mandates. Why don't they ignore BIS? Why do all these central banks of the world simply obey BIS even when it is detrimental to their economies? The central banks of the world sheepishly obey BIS because they are all private corporations owned by the same people who own BIS – specifically Rothchild family – and they do not care about the national economies or the people of the world: they only care about their profits and power.

After US markets (DJIA) reached 14000, an all-time high, new BIS rules called Besel II were imposed. Basel II required banks to adjust the value of their marketable securities to the "market price" of the security, a rule called "mark to market." Banks that were sufficiently well capitalized to make new loans were suddenly considered insolvent. That is, if they sold all their assets at that instant, they would have had less capital than was required by new rules of BIS. The new rules required that they assume that they sold all their assets at that moment. Financial analyst John Berlau: "The crisis is often called a 'market failure,' the mark-to-market rules are profoundly anti-market and hinder the free-market function of price discovery. . . . In this case, the accounting rules fail to allow the market players to hold on to an asset if they don't like what the market is currently fetching, an important market action that affects price discovery in areas from agriculture to antiques."

Imposing the mark-to-market rule on U.S. banks caused an instant credit freeze. That started destroying US economy and also economies of the rest of the world. In early April 2009, U.S. Financial Accounting Standards Board (FASB) overruled the BIS rules. So, US Government can intervene and change the BIS requirements, if it wants to. So can every sovereign governments in the world but the government officials are unaware of all this. BIS wins because of the ignorance of governments. The beauty of democracy is that the government is constituted by parliaments or House of Representatives elected to serve for a few years. These representatives need money to get elected. They will do the bidding of their financiers. Banks have money and they generously fund corrupt crooks to win elections. Those who get elected are usually not educated in international financial matters. Government will not notice how BIS, IMF, and Central banks ruin the country's economy. Manmohan Singh was an exception. He was educated in economics and knew how international bankers operate. But he was on the payroll of IMF. He opened up the Indian markets to foreign corporations including Monsanto, Big Pharma, Enron and Coca Cola, and privatized government enterprises and allowed foreign banks and insurance companies to come in. Rupee was devalued and became $1=Rs.69. Manmohan Singh brought in other IMF saboteurs like Duvvuri and Rajan (he was not even an economist) to govern RBI. Manmohan even proposed GST to give all the secret business data of all Indian businesses to foreign corporations through foreign-owned ICICI and HDFC banks. Then IMF brought in Modi, a religious bigot, was as PM to pit Muslims and Hindus against each other and destroy society.

It is obvious that BIS deliberately caused all this turmoil and devastation and crashed the world economy. But, why? The goal, it seems, was to create so much economic havoc that the world would panic and ditch their national currencies and accept the global currency privately-created by IMF and BIS. BIS and IMF work together as a team.

6 Evil Twins: IMF and WB

Representatives of the 41 winning nations of WWII – mainly USA and England – met in the name of United Nations Monetary and Financial conference, in the Mount Washington Hotel in Brettenwood, New Hampshire, USA, in July 1944. During this conference, IMF and World Bank were created for helping financially troubled nations. Federal Reserve Bank, the privately owned central bank of USA, is the 51% shareholder of both IMF and World Bank. In public statements, the 'US Treasury' is mentioned in place of 'Federal Reserve Bank', to give the public the impression that IMF is controlled by US Govt. But, IMF and World Bank are private Banks owned by Federal Reserve Bank and BoE and other private banks, which are in turn owned by Rothschild family.

According to IMF, it has currently 184 member countries. It was established to promote international monetary cooperation, exchange rate stability, and orderly exchange arrangements; and to provide temporary financial assistance to countries to help ease balance of payments adjustment. It is based in Washington DC. The managing director is a European Jew recommended by Federal Reserve Bank. Currently 75 countries owe the IMF 34 billion. Their operations include surveillance of member countries and world economy, technical assistance and financial support. The financial support is provided in the form of loans to which conditions are attached. These conditions are called 'conditionalities'. ... The founders aimed to build a framework for economic co-operation that would avoid a repetition of the disastrous economic policies that had contributed to the Great Depression of the 1930's and the global conflict that followed.... The financial aid given to a member country of IMF is always bound to so-called 'Conditionalities", including Structural Adjustment Programs (SAP). In many cases these conditionalities retard social stability, while Structural Adjustment Programs lead to an increase in poverty in recipient countries.'

According to Joseph Stiglitz, ex-chief economist of the World Bank, who talked to media in 2001, World Bank has designed an assistance strategy for every poor nation. World Bank officials and the officials of the poor nation always meet in a 5 star hotel. At the conclusion of the meeting, a begging finance minister is handed a 'restructuring agreement' pre-drafted for 'voluntary' signature. Each nation is given the same four-step program.

Step One: *Privatization. Rather than objecting to the sell-offs of state industries, some politicians - using the World Bank's demands to silence local critics - happily sold their electricity and water companies and pocketed huge commissions for shaving a few billion off the sale price.*

According to Stiglitz, who was a member of Bill Clinton's cabinet and chairman of the President's council of economic advisers, the US government knew it, at least in the case of the biggest privatization of all, the 1995 Russian sell-off. The US Treasury loved it and they engineered Yeltsin's re-election through a corrupt election. The US-backed oligarchs stripped Russia's industrial assets, with the effect that national output was cut in half.

Step Two: *Capital market liberalization. In theory this allows investment capital to flow in and out freely. Unfortunately, as in Indonesia and Brazil, two very rich countries which were stripped bare by IMF and World Bank, the money simply flows out. This is called 'hot money' cycle. Cash comes in for speculation in real estate and currency, and then flees before the bubble bursts. A nation's reserves can drain in days. In the case of Thailand, it was made a pauper state overnight by George Soros, a Rothchild. Then to seduce speculators into returning a nation's own capital funds, the IMF demands these nations raise interest rates to 30%, 50% and 80%. (This is the interest rates these nations will have to pay to get their capital to come back to their country.) Higher interest rates demolish property values, savage industrial production and drain national treasuries.*

Step Three: *market-based pricing which is a fancy term for raising prices on food, water and cooking gas. This leads, to 'the IMF riot'. When the IMF eliminated food and fuel subsidies for the poor in Indonesia in 1998, riots broke out in Indonesia. When water prices were increased by IMF, Bolivians rioted. When the price of cooking gas was increased by World Bank, Ecuador erupted into riots. The plan to make the US dollar Ecuador's currency has pushed 51% of the population below the poverty line. IMF and World Bank plans are calculated to cause 'social unrest'.*

The IMF riots are usually peaceful demonstrations but they are violently dispersed on advice of IMF and World Bank, by bullets, tanks and tear gas. These riots cause new flights of capital and government bankruptcies. During this economic arson, foreigners pick off remaining assets at fire sale prices. There are lots of losers but the clear winners are the western banks, and Federal Reserve Bank.

Step Four: *Free trade by the rules of the World Trade Organization and the World Bank. Americans kick down barriers to sales in Asia, Latin Americ and Africa while barricading its own markets against the Third World's agriculture. In the Opium Wars, to open the markets of China, the West used military blockades. Today, the World Bank can order a financial blockade, which is more effective and deadlier than military blockades .*

The IMF and World Bank plans undermine democracy and devastate the target country. Under the guidance of IMF structural 'assistance' program (SAP), Africa's income dropped by 23%. Botswana kicked out IMF and managed to avoid that fate. The Oligarchs who acquired most of the land in the target countries rents the land out for agriculture to locals and collect 50% of the crop as rent. Zimbabwe, once known as the Jewel of Africa, enacted land redistribution laws and gave land back to farmers. But, then the international bankers ruined their economy and made their currency worthless and forced them to accept US dollar as their national currency. IMF and World Bank would suck every last drop of blood out of their target country.

One of the main IMF-SAP conditions placed on troubled countries is that the governments sell up as much of their national assets as they can, to western corporations at heavily discounted prices. This cripples the societies within the troubled countries. Brazil is an example. The western corporations have swallowed up the food production industry there. All food produced in the country is exported to pay for the debt the country owe to foreign banks. Now Brazilians are starving to death, even though Brazil is the world's biggest exporter of food.

In 1987 Edmond de Rothchild created the World Conservation Bank. It is designed to transfer debts from third world countries to this bank. In return, those countries would give land to this bank. This would give Rothschild control of the third world which represents 30% of the land surface of the Earth.

IMF has a new tactic to impose its own currency on all nations: it will confess that it has been evil in the past, but learned its lessons and promise to be good in the future, and then offer a world currency as solution for all those evils. The 'brettenwoodsproject [dot] org' web site now says that the IMF system is "a problematic system". An article dated September 2009 tells us how 'poorly governed IMF system has created enormous problems for the world, and for developing countries in particular. "First: it creates a volatile, risky environment for business investment. Even in times of relative global stability, volatile exchange rates damage economic planning and investment in rich and poor countries alike. If there is a lack of stability in exchange rates over the medium to long-term, where effective markets to hedge risks do not exist, businesses must expect volatility and incorporate that risk into their plans. Investment will be lower, because investments which might be profitable with stable exchange rates will either be unprofitable when risks are included in planning, or not undertaken by risk-averse investors. This reduces job creation, growth, trade and economic development. This is a particular concern given the enormous long term investments that will be required to convert our economies to a low-carbon future. Ultimately exchange rate volatility mainly benefits speculators, while creating enormous costs.

Second: the current international monetary system creates enormous risks for small or poor countries that are extremely vulnerable to swings in their exchange rates. In times of crises, they are often forced to devalue their currencies, increasing the cost of servicing foreign debts and making imports, including essential food stuffs more expensive. The small size of the markets in most developing countries' currencies makes them targets for speculation and manipulation of their currencies.

Third: there are significant direct costs for the governments of developing countries. Developing countries have accumulated large stashes of foreign currency reserves partly to provide sufficient funds to prevent them from having to turn to the IMF should they need to protect their currencies or stabilize their balance of payments. Holding large reserves means tying up assets that could otherwise be used for investment in green infrastructure, education, health, environmental management or other activities which have long-run benefits for sustainable development.

Fourth: since the collapse of the Bretton Woods system in the early 1970's (when America refused to return the gold that was deposited with them by other countries), there has been a proliferation of costly and destabilizing financial crises, culminating in the current debacle, described by the UN as 'the worst financial and economic crisis since the great depression.' "

IMF and WB were created to avoid instability. Instead, they have

created instability. Now, they say they have a solution to all these problems which they created: "the creation of an international currency, international clearing union, and system of globally managed exchange rates.'
(www.brettonwoodsproject.org/institution/imf). Or, in other words, IMF and WB created all these financial havoc in this world to prepare the way for the creation of a world with 'one fascist government and one currency' run by Rothchild.

Hungary became the first European Country to ban Rothschild's IMF Banks on July 20, 2016. This was in response to meddling in the country's affairs by IMF and EU. The PM Victor Orban promised to pay off the money owed to IMF by end of year. However, within month, Hungary paid off the loan owed to IMF saving €11.7 million worth of interest expenses. (IMF did not allow India to pay off its loan early. India had to pay all the interest that was originally expected to be paid over the life of the loan.) IMF claimed that it was setup to provide economic growth and stability to the governments. However, people have noticed that one of its main goals is to commit the governments to more borrowing programs in exchange to political and economic concessions.

It was the poor economic policies of the United States and the Western economies in general which forced countries like Hungary to borrow from the IMF and other Rothschild banks. They make millions of dollars in interest from the poor and crumbling economies. By doing so, Rothschild extends its influence on the governments and literally controls them.

Orban's predecessor borrowed from the IMF. When Victor Orban came to power, he changed the constitution and decided to ease off austerity measures that were mandated by IMF conditionalities. International press, which is owned by Bankers, has been calling Orban a dictator and anti-democratic ever since. Since Hungary is a NATO member and a Christian European country, it may not be attacked militarily like Libya, Iraq and Syria were attacked, at least not immediately. IMF and Rothschild never forget a hurt. Many people expect Orban to be eventually murdered or poisoned or infected with non-curable cancer like they did with Yasser Arafat and Hugo Chavez and Muammar Kaddafi and Saddam Hussein.

Here are what some internet bloggers wrote:

"Expect a false-flag attack with Hungary as a scapegoat and/or hear excessive propaganda about them aiding anti-western freedom endeavors. Almost every conflict after the 70's was about a country not accepting the U.S. central banking system (eternal debt).
First they try to bribe the dictators of those countries into taking out loans they can't afford. If they agree, the country uses its natural resources as collateral and let corporations setup shop and the country's citizens become debt slaves. If they disagree, they are assassinated in the name of 'freedom' by a government agency or someone they pay (Economic Hitmen). Then the US causes complete havoc behind the scenes to justify their occupation, but never actually takes over the region. They would rather have puppets do it for them and give off the illusion that the US government is just helping the poor country get back on their feet and help themselves. Gotta fight dat terrorism, you know, the thing that kills less people than food allergies, or obesity, or smoking or dog bites. Then they use scare mongering as a means to convince the people to relinquish their rights in exchange for security."

"The central banks were started in Europe by the Rothschilds. The U.S. is no doubt the destroyer of nations to create central banks but our politicians tried fighting the notion of a central bank until a few politicians sold us out in the early 20th century. So, in essence it's now a U.S. central banking system but it started in Europe. Speaking of puppets, the U.S. is nothing but a (major) puppet controlled by a globalist shadow government."

"Hungary will have 'freedom bombs' dropped on them at some point. When the Germans cracked down on Jewish banking in the late 1920s and early 1930s there were New York Times articles with the title "all Judes declares war on Germany" referring to the economic boycott and

increased pressure on them from other states. Look at how Vladimir Putin is being pushed to war as we speak."

"What I suspect is that there will be some form of retaliation against Hungary. Maybe not a war though. But there are plenty of other ways IMF/Rothschild can hit the Hungarians.
One likely possibility is that Hungary will experience a bunch of economic woes, inflation, currency collapse, trade disputes etc."

"The ECB are criminals who have ravaged southern Europe, by causing the money supply to contract by 33% between 2010 and 2014.
(http://www.tradingeconomics.com/greece/money-supply-m1).
Tight money is the cause of most of southern Europe's woes.
Why do I sense war coming to hungry very soon?"

"USA is building a NATO-Belt against Russia and Hungary is part of this. A war against Hungary would break NATO. They will deal with Hungary later. Most likely through some sort of economic bullying."

"Looks like Hungary needs a strong dose of 'freedom'. Prepare the murder machine! Don't forget to pay your tithe to your slave master, you have to buy your 'freedom' with your citizenship. Besides, I see a 'populist uprising' coming to Hungary in the near future."

"Victor Orban is a BAD MAN. So, whatever shall we do to FIX this "problem"? Kill a few million innocent Hungarian civilians, like we did to "fix" the "problem" with Saddam?
Welp, looks like Hungary is trying to start a war. We might have to go in and spread some 'democracy' around."

"Gaddafi was portrayed as a "brutal dictator" who gave his soldiers viagra to mass rape his people. Yet the people cheered him as he moved among them without security. Imagine this in any western democracy. When Gaddafi was ruler of Libya: 'there is no electricity bill in Libya; electricity is free for all its citizens.
There is no interest on loans, banks in Libya are state-owned and loans given to all its citizens at zero percent interest by law.
Having a home considered a human right in Libya.
All newlyweds in Libya receive $60,000 dinar (U.S.$50,000) by the government to buy their first apartment so to help start up the family.

Education and medical treatments are free in Libya. Before Gaddafi, only 25 percent of Libyans were literate. Today, the figure is 83 percent. Should Libyans want to take up farming career, they would receive farming land, a farming house, equipments, seeds and livestock to kickstart their farms, all for free.
If Libyans cannot find the education or medical facilities they need, the government funds them to go abroad, for it is not only paid for, but they get a U.S.$2,300/month for accommodation and car allowance.
If a Libyan buys a car, the government subsidizes 50 percent of the price. The price of petrol in Libya is $0.14 per liter.
Libya has no external debt and its reserves amounting to $150 billion are now frozen globally.
If a Libyan is unable to get employment after graduation the state would pay the average salary of the profession, as if he or she is employed, until employment is found.
A portion of every Libyan oil sale is credited directly to the bank accounts of all Libyan citizens.
A mother who gives birth to a child receive U.S.$5,000.
40 loaves of bread in Libya costs $0.15.
25 percent of Libyans have a university degree."

US and Europe sent their mercenary proxy army to effect 'regime change' and dropped 'freedom bombs' on Libya and turned that country into a pile of rubble and liberated it from 'so called brutal dictatorship'. Today Libya is western democracy.
At least two political bodies claim to be the government of Libya. The Council of Deputies is internationally recognized as the legitimate government, but it does not hold territory in the capital, Tripoli, instead meeting in the Cyrenaica city of Tobruk. Meanwhile, the 2014 General National Congress purports to be the legal continuation of the General National Congress, elected in the 2012 Libyan General National Congress election and dissolved following the June 2014 elections but then reconvened by a minority of its members. The Supreme Court in Tripoli declared the Tobruk government unconstitutional in November 2014, but the internationally recognized government has rejected the ruling as made under threat of violence. Parts of Libya are outside of either government's control, with various Islamist, rebel, and tribal militias administering some cities and areas."

"The mainstream media told us that there was an opposition to Gaddafi.

But those with the regime change agenda couldn't find or create local opposition. So, they had to bring in 250,000 foreign mercenaries. (http://libyanwarthetruth.com/who-are-james-and-joanne-moriarty-our-story-intro)."

When IMF and World Bank come into a country, the country is forced to open up the markets to American and Western countries. At the same time those countries' exports to USA and West are blocked. But, sometimes a little bribe to the policy makers of the country can do the job. Manmohan Singh was the RBI chairman and then the Prime minister of India. During his period in office, he opened up India for Western corporations under the terms of WTO. His successor, Mr. Modi who was elected with help of American and Israeli spies and subversive agents cloaked as NGOs working inside India, passed GST and signed military pacts with US Military and appointed IMF agents as RBI chairman and RBI board members and as economic advisors to PM and practically surrendered the country to Western Banks. Foreigners achieved all this with a little bribe to key decision makers in India.

7 World Currency

On April 7, 2009, 'The London Telegraph' declared: 'The G20 Moves the World a Step Closer to a Global Currency'. "A clause in Point 19 of the communiqué issued by the G20 leaders read: 'We have agreed to support a general SDR allocation which will inject $250 billion into the world economy and increase global liquidity'. SDR (Special Drawing Rights) is a paper currency issued by the IMF without any gold or other backing.

This declaration by the G20 leaders has activated the IMF's power to create money. This is making SDRs, the global currency backed by a global central bank, running monetary policy for all humanity. It is outside the control of any sovereign body. Later when the world's central bankers met in Washington, they discussed and decided that BIS is most capable to carry out that awesome and fearful responsibility.

Or, in other words, BIS is trying to replace all national currencies with SDRs of IMF. But, will Russia and China and India and America ditch their currencies and accept SDRs? Not right away. But they will, under conditions of extreme distress. Europe had many nations and each nation had its own currency and its own Rothchild-owned central bank. Various small wars and then WWI and WWII devastated their economy. In that weakened condition, they were ready to accept a common currency to avoid future wars and further devastation. Rothchild opened a new bank for the entire Europe called ECB. They printed their own currency called Euro and it was accepted by all the countries of Europe. ECB is not under the jurisdiction of any sovereign country. It is independent and nobody can question its actions. It functions like all other Rothchild banks: it prints paper money (it is commonly called 'fiat' money because it is not backed by gold or any other valuables) and lends it to governments and other banks for 6% interest. The interest and principal need to be repaid in gold or silver. By increasing the money in circulation, ECB creates inflation and economic boom. Then, by reducing the amount of money in circulation, ECB creates mass unemployment and social unrest and bankruptcies. Rothchild banks and corporations move in and swoop up all the banks and businesses and resources at pennies on the dollar. Through boom and bust cycles, ECB ruins Europe just like FED does in USA.

First, EU gave money liberally to all these countries for unnecessary but nice infrastructure development. Then ECB contracted the money supply by 33% between 2010 and 2014. Spain, Ireland, Portugal, Greece, Cypress and Iceland were on brink of bankruptcy. Unemployment and bankruptcies soared and property values plummeted. Then then these countries were directed to IMF to straighten out their financial mess. IMF generously loaned its SDRs to these countries to make up for the reduced money supply, and they loaned them beyond their ability to repay. But IMF loans come with conditionalities. IMF required that these countries reduce support to poor and retirees and privatize medical care and government-owned industries. This created more misery. Then IMF required these countries to increase taxation and to implement austerity programs and put down any social unrest violently. They required them to open up their borders and allow immigration into the country from poor nations like Africa. They required them to open up the markets and shut down domestic production and allow American corporations to buy domestic companies and sell their products. They required them to allow Monsanto to sell GMO seeds and legalize GMO products without identifying labeling. They required them to legalize abortion to reduce population growth and mandate vaccination of all pregnant women and new-born children with American vaccines to increase autism rate among the children. Currently 1 in 10 children in America are autistic due to tainted vaccines. Soon the rate will climb to 1 in 2 children. They required them to criminalize Islam and expel Muslims. They required them to make criticizing Israel a crime, and enact thought crime laws to eradicate any thought unfavorable to Jews and Israel. They may add more demands as time goes on. IMF and World Bank work together and every country that receive IMF and WB loans are put on the same four step program.

When these countries fail to pay the loans, they will be forced to accept even more loans at higher interest rates and impose even more misery upon the population. Iceland declared bankruptcy and it expelled its central bank directors and refused to repay ECB loans. Well, any country that refuse to pay back IMF, ECB, FED, WB, or BIS loans will be declared undemocratic dictatorship. To liberate the population from undemocratic dictatorship, America and NATO will start dropping freedom bombs on these countries and turn it into a pile of rubble and kill a few million citizens before a peace treaty is signed and make them pay back even more than what they initially had to pay. So, Iceland wisely paid back their IMF loans.

Greece rebelled and refused to pay back the IMF loans. Then IMF engineered a regime change and got one of their agents elected as PM. He agreed to pay back IMF loans and take even more loans from IMF at even higher interest rates and imposed even tighter austerity programs on its citizens.

Now, through the creation of ECB, 19 of the 28 European countries have accepted one common currency - ECB Euro. Asian countries are expected to be brought under one financial union, like EU. African countries are expected to be brought under another financial union. Each of these financial unions will have their own Rothchild central bank like ECB. Then through increasing and then decreasing money supply, the member nations will be ruined. Their economies will be devastated and there will be great social unrest and even WWIII. Then the currencies of these financial unions will be replaced by IMF SDRs.

Creation of a trade block with USA, Canada and Mexico, under the

North American Free Trade Agreement (NAFTA) was the first step before implementing a common currency called Amero. FED's Amero will be the future common currency for USA, Canada, Mexico and other countries in the American continent that might join NAFTA. In Europe, first Rothchild bankers created a common trade block called European Common Market. Then they created a political cooperation called European Union (EU). Then Rothchild created a central bank called ECB. Then all member nations replaced their national currencies with Euro issued by ECB. Modus operandi is same. Similar moves are being made among the Asian countries and among African Union countries. It was originally rumored that Amero will replace dollars in 2016. But the introduction is delayed.

As of 2016, in America, every man woman and child owes $68000 to the FED. This is called the national debt. That means holders of each of the 300 shares of FED is owed 74 Billion dollars. This is in addition to the hundreds of billions of dollars each of them earned for their shares already. Pretty good return on investment.

Iran, Syria, Iraq, Afghanistan, Cuba, North Korea and Libya did not have a Rothchild-owned central bank. Rothchild made a decision to impose his central bank upon them. American army is the enforcer arm of IMF and WB and BIS. The bankers set up a false-flag operation called '9/11 incident in NY' and used it as excuse to send American forces into these countries. America turned Afghanistan, Iraq, Libya, and Syria into piles of rubble and killed millions of people and set up Rothchild Central banks. America had to borrow money from FED to satisfy the wishes of Rothchild - viz. establishing Rothchild banks in those countries. Total cost to USA is estimated at 6 trillion dollars. This, at a time when USA has no money for its schools or its roads or its welfare programs. It has been reported that Mr. Rothchild and his new wife slept in Lincoln bedroom in the White House on September 10th and on September 11th they watched the fireworks from their hotel room overlooking the 'twin towers'. The controlled demolition of 'twin towers' was a spectacular fireworks display fit for Sir Edmond Rothchild on his honeymoon.

Even countries with powerful armies, nuclear weapons and patriotic fervor will ditch their national currencies and accept a world currency, when they are totally destroyed by war, like in Afghanistan, Iraq, Libya and Syria. Vanquished will accept anything dictated by the victors. WWIII is just around the corner.

8. Experts Recommend New World Currency

Rothschild central banks engineered a financial crisis in 2008. Then all the vultures (experts) came out of the wood work. Functional definition of an 'Expert' is: 'someone with a PhD from an American University which teaches corporate-designed crooked economics.' All the experts assume that national political leaders are incapable of handling their own financial affairs and that national economies are doomed and a world currency is needed to protect the world from global calamity. Based on these assumptions, they proclaim: "With an unwillingness to accept dollars and the absence of an alternative, international payments system can go into a freeze beyond the control of monetary authorities leading the world economy into a Great Depression, ... In order to avoid such a calamity, the international community should immediately revive the idea of the Substitution Account mooted in 1971, under which official holders of dollars can deposit their unwanted dollars in a special account in the IMF with the values of deposits denominated in an international currency such as the SDR of the IMF." Or, in other words, 'the sky is falling, the sky is falling, everybody give up your currencies.'

Such discussions of a new global currency have led to fears of a falling dollar. But, FED is capable of supporting itself. FED started massive QE and flooded the world at the rate of almost a trillion dollars every month.

In 1998, Jeffrey Garten, a member of the Council on Foreign Relations, wrote: "over time the United States set up crucial ... Federal Reserve (1913). In so doing, America became a managed national economy. .. to make capitalism work, to prevent destructive business cycles and to moderate the harsh, invisible hand of Adam Smith... This is what now must occur on a global scale. The world needs an institution that has a hand on the economic rudder when the seas become stormy. It needs a global central bank."

Dr. William Overholt, senior research fellow at Harvard's Kennedy School, formerly with the Rand Institute: "To avoid another crisis, we need an ability to manage global liquidity. Theoretically that could be achieved through some kind of global central bank, or through the creation of a global currency, or through global acceptance of a set of rules with sanctions and a dispute settlement mechanism."

Guillermo Calvo, Professor of Economics, International and Public Affairs at Columbia University, in 2009: the 20th century saw the creation of national or regional central banks in charge of a subset of the capital market. It has now become apparent that the realm of existing central banks is very limited and the world has no institution that fulfills the necessary global role. The IMF is moving in that direction, but it is still too small and too limited to adequately do so."

In November 2008, it was reported that Baron David de Rothschild visited the Middle East, and he told: "I shares most people's view that there is a new world order. … there will be a new form of global governance."

Robert Zoellick, President of the World Bank (April of 2009): "If leaders are serious about creating new global governance, let them start by empowering the WTO, the IMF, and the World Bank Group to monitor national policies."

Gideon Rachman, a Bilderberger: ".. the European Union has already set up a continental government for 27 countries, which could be a model. The EU has a supreme court, a currency, thousands of pages of law, a large civil service and the ability to deploy military force.".. the European model could "go global"… as the financial crisis and climate change are pushing national governments towards global solutions"

These vultures expect a Pan Asian union and an Asian currency unit as a third reserve on the model of EU, by 2025. These experts say democracy is a hindrance to creation of NWO. So, a new world government with a world currency will be forged with a totalitarian, authoritarian global government structure. The concept of a global currency and global central bank is authoritarian in its very nature, as it removes any vestiges of oversight and accountability away from the people of the world, and toward a small, group of international elites, specifically Rothschild family.

The proposed solution to the current so-called global financial crisis benefit those who created the crisis, and the middle classes, the world's dispossessed, poor, and indebted people will continue to suffer.

So, the lackeys of the Rothschild all agree that there should be a 'new world order' in finance operated by Rothchilds. These knaves and saboteurs of national economies are given Nobel prizes, for such views.

Timothy Geithner, head of the New York Federal Reserve (June 2008): "Banks and investment banks .. should operate under a unified regulatory framework, .. the US Federal Reserve should play a "central role" in the new regulatory framework." So, America wants to be the big dog. Let us look at how America does its banking.

9 Money and Banking in USA

The Constitution of the USA: Article 1, Section 8:

"The Congress shall have power: To lay and collect Taxes, Duties, Imposts and Excises, to pay the Debts and provide for the common defense and general Welfare of the United States; but all Duties, Imposts and Excises shall be uniform throughout the United States;
To borrow Money on the credit of the United States;
To regulate Commerce with foreign Nations, and among the several States, and with the Indian Tribes;
To establish an uniform Rule of Naturalization, and uniform Laws on the subject of Bankruptcies throughout the United States;
To coin Money, regulate the Value thereof, and of foreign Coin, and fix the Standard of Weights and Measures;
To provide for the Punishment of counterfeiting the Securities and current coin of the United States;.."

Thomas Jefferson: "I believe that banking institutions are more dangerous to our liberties than standing armies.... Already they have raised up a money aristocracy that has set the government at defiance. The issuing power (of money), should be taken from the banks and restored to the people to whom it properly belongs." The American Revolution was a struggle to wrest control of wealth from the Bank of England and to restore the centers of power to the People. The constitution is clear about where the power belongs.

Benjamin Franklin said that the inability of the colonists to get the power to issue their own money permanently out of the hands of George III and the international bankers was the prime reason for the Revolutionary War.

Thomas Jefferson: "If the American people ever allow private banks to control the issue of currency, first by inflation, then by deflation, the banks and corporations that will grow up around them will deprive the people of all property until their children will wake up homeless on the continent their fathers conquered."

John Adams: "All the perplexities, confusions, and distresses in America arise, not from defects in the Constitution or confederation, not from want of honor or virtue, as much as from downright ignorance of the nature of coin, credit, and circulation".

Rothchild: "Those that create and issue money and credit direct the policies of government and hold in their hands the destiny of the people".

Adams, Jefferson and Lincoln believed that banker capitalism was more dangerous to our liberties than standing armies. In a republic, banks would lend money but could not create or manufacture it.

Jefferson: the 'Central Bank' is "one of the most deadly enemies of the principles and form of our Constitution." Jefferson did not want to deliver our monetary system into private hands to be run for private profit.

President James A. Garfield: "Whoever controls the money in any country is absolute master of industry, legislation and commerce".

Thomas Jefferson expected the government to control its money, and incur no debt unlike in the European system.

Rothschilds: 'whoever controls the issuance of money controls the government.'

There have been two ways to issue new currency: (1) The government prints the money, debt-free and interest-free, and circulate it through the economy for use as a medium of exchange. There is no tax levied on the public to pay interest on the currency in circulation because it is debt-and-interest-free. This is the system Jefferson demanded. Lincoln used it with his "greenbacks" and got killed for it. Kennedy desired it and got killed for it.

(2) The Citizens allow the bank to print cash. The bank pays printing costs. The Citizens do not charge the bank any interest for use of the printed currency.

The bank uses the cash to buy government bond which pays interest. The bank keeps some of the bonds and sells some of the bonds to the public for a fee. The bank can buy back the bonds from the public simply by printing more money.

The bankers can create inflation and depressions by manipulating the amount of currency in circulation. It also prints money and uses this printed money to buy loans from other banks. Such money creates inflation.

Citizens give the bank cash without charging interest. They charge Citizens interest on their own currency. This is how the Central Banks operate.

Benjamin Franklin explained why the colonies thrived: "That is simple. In the colonies we issue our own money. It is called Colonial Scrip. We issue it in proper proportions to the demands of trade and industry." Colonial Scrip had no debt or interest attached."

Alexander Hamilton, with the help of international bankers, started Bank of America in 1781 to keep the country under the influence of bankers. The prosperity that was achieved with "Colonial Scrip" money was wiped out in a few years by the bank money.

Benjamin Franklin: "Conditions were so reversed that the era of prosperity had ended and a depression set in to such an extent that the streets of the Colonies were filled with the unemployed!" Bank money had debt and interest attached. Hamilton converted the interest-free public debt into interest bearing bonds payable to his bank. That is what private central banks do.

Hamilton's bank charter expired in 1811. In 1812, international bankers instigated a war between England and its colonies. When there is a war, the government will need large amounts of money and it will be forced to borrow from private banks. That is how it has been in Europe. American colonies went to war with England and it lasted until 1816. Star spangled Banner was written and Colonies were euphoric over its victories. In 1816, a private central bank was started with $35 million capital. Government put in 7 million. It issued currency with debt and interest attached to it. Throughout history, interest based currency has always led to depression. The colonies suffered a major depression. The charter of the bank expired in 1836. President Andrew Jackson vetoed its renewal and said: "The Bank is trying to kill me - but I will kill it! .... If the American people only understood the rank injustice of our money and banking system - there would be a revolution before morning..." So, America had no central bank and the economy thrived. The frustrated central bankers instigated and financed the Civil War. President Lincoln needed money to fight the war. The international bankers offered him loans at 24-36% interest. Lincoln balked at their demands because he didn't want to plunge the nation into such a huge debt.

Lincoln thought it was ridiculous to borrow paper money from bankers at such high interest rates when US Treasury can just as well print paper money without paying any interest. He asked Congress to pass a law to authorize the printing of U.S. Treasury Notes. Lincoln said "We gave the people of this Republic the greatest blessing they ever had - their own paper money to pay their debts..." Lincoln printed over 400 million debt-free, interest-free dollars called "Greenbacks". Lincoln paid the soldiers and government employees with it. He bought war supplies with it. When International Bankers failed to indebt the nation with huge war loans at high interest rates, they conspired and assassinated Lincoln.

Lincoln's vice President, who was in on the conspiracy to assassinate him, became President and he revoked the Greenback law. A new national banking act was enacted and all money became interest bearing again. It is against common sense why Government would let a private entity to print money and pay interest on it when government can print the same money without paying interest. But, politicians who receive huge bribes from Rothchild Bankers would do things against common sense and detrimental to the country. Money talks. Many government insiders and associates of Lincoln were part of the Rothschild's' conspiracy to assassinate Lincoln.

Thomas A Edison: "If our nation can issue a dollar bond (interest-bearing) it can issue a dollar bill (interest-free). The element that makes the bond good makes a bill good also. The difference between the bond and the bill is that the bond lets money-brokers collect twice the amount of the bond and an additional 20 percent, whereas the currency pays nobody but those who contribute directly in some useful way. It is absurd to say that our country can issue $30 million in bonds and not $30 million in currency. Both are promises to pay: but one promise fattens the usurers (interest-collectors) and the other helps the people."

The International Bankers (Rothchild bankers) conspired and financed the election campaigns of senators and congressmen and President, and in return they promised to pass the Federal Reserve bank act. Those congressmen and senators passed the Federal Reserve Bank Act in 1913, when majority of congressmen and senators were away for Christmas.

The corporate-financed American Universities teach its students that only banks can print money and that money has to be borrowed at high interest rate from banks. Even though interest-bearing currency has always led to depressions, they are taught in universities that when government prints interest-free money it will lead to hyper-inflation. The students are taught not to use their own common sense and realize that government can print money without causing hyper-inflation and depressions and massive unemployment. President Lincoln has proved it.

Bankers buy up the universities and Professors and publishers of text books and mass communication media in addition to funding election campaigns. In America the mainstream media is completely owned by Bankers. So, only voices supporting an interst-bearing private cental banking system are allowed to be printed or broadcast. Bankers are very good in silencing people with opposing view points. If they cannot be bribed and bought, they will be deprived of a job and income and then if still not controlled, they will be killed by suicides, accidents, poisonings and assassinations.

On June 4, 1964, President Kennedy issued Executive Order 11110. This Executive Order called for the issuance of new debt-free, interest-free currency - the United States Note - through US Treasury bypassing FED. The central bankers were furious and they conspired and assassinated Kennedy. At the time, $4.2 billion of this currency was put into circulation. Kennedy's vice President who was in on the conspiracy to assassinate him, became President and before Kennedy's body turned cold, withdrew the executive order 11110 verbally. Kennedy's treasury notes were withdrawn from circulation. If continued, it would have eliminated the FED and saved the country from the huge national debt. The national debt stands at 22.4 trillion in 2016.

When interest-free treasury notes are used, the government has less interest expenses. When expenses are less, taxes will be less. When taxes are less people can spend more of their money to buy more. That will lead to higher demand and higher production and higher employment. But if the government or the central bank print money without increasing production, it will result in hyper-inflation, as happened in Germany.

The interest paid on the money borrowed from central bank keeps increasing as the quantity of money in circulation increase. Government will have to increase tax to pay the higher interest. As people spend more of their income for taxes, they will buy less. Then demand will decrease and production will decrease and that will reduce employment. When the production decrease, with the same amount of money in circulation, inflation will increase. Inflation will reduce the buying power of the dollar. It is a vicious cycle.

In 2015, 75 % of all the income tax collected was used for paying interest on the money borrowed from FED. That leaves less money for other government activities like building roads and schools. So, government has to borrow even more from FED. Within a few years, all the money collected from taxes will be used strictly for paying interest to FED. Government will become bankrupt. FED bankers will legally own the nation, the houses, the cars, the businesses and everything else, just as Thomas Jefferson predicted. At that point the government will not be able to function; the government will collapse under the debt load; there will be massive unemployment and chaos. The FED knows about this and has made plans for dealing with the situation. The congressmen and senators and president whose election campaigns were financed by FED, have already passed necessary laws to control the crowds and establish a fascist authoritarian government. FEMA has already bought four billion hollowpoint bullets specially made for sniper shooting of people, and 1.5 billion plastic coffins to bury all the people who are going to be culled when the riots break out. Several FEMA camps have been prepared to intern the survivors until they can be re-programmed and put into productive use or killed off. Mass killings or culling as bankers call it, is part of Rothschild's agenda for New World Order. They want to reduce the world population to 500 million as declared in the 'Georgia Guidestones'.

10. Federal Reserve Bank

In theory, banks are in the business of taking in money from depositors for interest and then loaning most of that money out to borrowers at a higher interest rate. The interest they receive from the borrowers is more than the interest they pay to depositors. The difference is their profit. Part of the profit will be used for cost of doing the business, like salaries, rent etc.

Money is a promise to pay. Banks can issue promissory notes to several customers based on same deposit. Banks were allowed to lend out 100 for every 6 in deposit. That means only a fraction of the loan amount will be kept as reserve by the bank. It is called 'fractional reserve banking'. For every 6 dollars in deposit, the bank will give out 100 dollars in loans. This works because those who take loans do not always take out cash and keep it under their pillows.

By law, banks are allowed to create money based on its reserves. The current reserve requirement is 6%. In other words, for every 6 dollars on deposit and held in reserve, the bank can create up to 94 additional dollars for the purpose of lending. That is 15 dollars for every dollar in deposit. This is called fractional reserve banking.

The banks used to pay around 1.5% interest on deposits. Now, it is 0.0002 % (practically 0%). Let us assume for the sake of example, that the bank pays 2% interest on deposit. Then it give out loans at, let's say, 7% interest. The bank will collect 7% interest on each of those 15 dollars loaned out. That means, based on each dollar placed on deposit, the bank will collect 97% in interest. After paying the original depositor the generous 2%, the bank actually receives a brokerage fee of approximately 95%. This shows how profitable this fractional reserve banking is.

If large number of depositors ask for their money back, the target bank will have to borrow money from other banks to pay them. If other banks refuse to lend money or are unable to lend money, the target bank will not be able to return the depositors' money immediately. It will have to call its loans back, which is a time consuming process. The only option would be for the target bank to close or declare bankruptcy. International bankers are all members or relatives of the Rothschild family. They work together and help each other like a pack of wolves and make sure their banks do not go bankrupt.

New York bankers have always been trying to establish a private central bank in America, just like they did in European countries. The first step was to create a crisis in banking. It was easy in those days. Depositors make large deposits in a target bank and then worthy clients will take loans from the bank. Then the depositors withdraw their deposits and close their accounts. The banks would not be able to re-call their loans in such a short notice. That means some depositors won't get their money immediately, even though the bank is solvent and profitable. The newspapers which are owned by the conspiring banks will publicize the fact that a customer was unable to withdraw his money from the target bank. Then the depositors panic and they all ask for their money. That is called a 'run on the bank'. The bank, unable to pay all depositors at once, will close.

In October of 1907, the conspiring Jewish Bankers spread rumors that Knickerbocker Trust Company of New York, a non-Jewish bank, was insolvent. It was very solvent. Depositors waited in line in front of the Knickerbocker bank to close their accounts and the Bank failed. Then, the rumors were spread that the Trust Company of America, a non-Jewish bank, was insolvent. Depositors withdrew their money and that Bank collapsed. Then the run on the bank spread to the Lincoln Trust Company, a non-Jewish bank. That also failed. Across the country depositors panicked and there were runs on various banks. The country went into recession. The banks owned by Rothchilds were not affected.

George F. Baker, president of the First National Bank, and James Stillman, president of National City Bank, and financier J. Pierpont Morgan presented themselves as the saviors of the banking industry. They offered loans to banks which they deemed solvent. The secretary of the treasury George B. Cortelyou offered government funds to the Bankers to prevent an economic disaster. President Theodore Roosevelt, a Jew who was elected with the financial help of Jewish bankers (usually referred to as international bankers), was conveniently on a hunting trip in Louisiana while all this happened.

J. P. Morgan decided which firms would fail and which would survive. He organized rescues of banks and trust companies he pleased and averted a shutdown of the New York Stock Exchange. When people take money out of one bank, they receive a check for their deposit amount, and they deposit it into another bank which they believe is solvent. So, the money that was taken out of the target bank was deposited into, let us say, JP Morgan's bank. JP Morgan will accept the check and give a receipt for the deposit. As long as the check was accepted by JP Morgan as a valid check, the depositor was happy. Thus, in the end, the panic was stopped and J.P.Morgan and Henry P. Davison and Benjamin Strong Jr. were recognized as the heroes for their work in organizing personnel and determining the liquidity of the banks involved in the crises. People did not notice that all these hero bankers were either members of the Rothschild family or connected to the Rothschild family by marriage or on the payroll of the Rothschild family.

After the 1907 panic, Congress formed the National Monetary Commission to review banking policies in the United States and make a recommendation to prevent future runs on banks. Senator Nelson W. Aldrich of Rhode Island was the chairman of the committee. He was the maternal uncle of the Rockefellers. He was believed to be a corrupt Jew on the payroll of the New York bankers. Aldrich toured Europe to learn about their banking systems. He decided that the answer was to create a private central bank like the BoE.

In November of 1910, Senator Aldrich and Rothchild bankers and their economic scholars assembled in a secret conference on Jekyll Island in Georgia. There, they conspired to create a private Rothschild-owned central bank in the image of BoE. The public hated Jewish owned New York Banks. So, this had to be a new Bank which is owned by Government, by the people, for the people and of the people. People were against European style central bank. All European central banks were owned by ruthless European Jews, specifically Rothschild family. These central banks have devastated Europe over decades by instigating and then financing wars between kingdoms and by increasing and then contracting money supply and thereby causing economic depressions and devastations and destabilizing their economies through fraud and usury. So, the new bank had to be a group of banks instead of one central bank. People were against banks issuing paper money without anything to back it and thereby causing runaway inflation and massive losses to public. So the new currency had to be either gold coins or bank notes that are exchangeable for gold. In either case the bank had to have gold in reserve. After about 10 days of brain storming, the conspirators created the perfect name to deceive the public: Federal Reserve Bank.

Federal implies that it is owned by Federal Government. Reserve indicates that it has gold reserve against which currency is issued. That means the new bank should raise enough capital from wealthy unnamed private entities with vast gold holdings. The FED will be governed by a committee and its chairman will be appointed by Government. To avoid concentration of power, the governance and ownership of the FED will be distributed among 12 regional independent FEDs. The regional FEDs will be owned by its member banks. These regional FEDs will be administered by committees selected by member banks.

So, the Federal Reserve Bank would be the new bank owned by all the banks – in essence of the banks, for the banks, by the banks – and it will have gold in reserve to print or mint currencies and it will be controlled by federal government. To make sure the FED will remain above the partisan politics, FED will be separate from and independent of the government and will not be subject to or governed by any government agencies. Financial security of the country is more important than partisan politics, of course. The governing committee of the FED would be appointed by the regional FEDs. President of the country would select a chairman from the list submitted to him by the FED. What could be more democratic, more anti-central-bank, and more government owned than the FED? Thus, the outer appearance of the Federal Reserve Bank was designed to be appealing and acceptable to the general public.

The devil is in the details. The details were very sinister, vicious, cunning, deceptive and destructive. All the attendees of the conspiracy, including Senator Aldrich, were agents of Rothchilds. Senator Nelson Aldrich was maternal grandfather to the Rockefellers. All the major New York banks were owned by Rothchilds family. The economists and banking and legal experts who attended the conspiracy were on the payroll of Rothschild's. What they wanted and what they designed was a Rothschild-owned central bank to control and usurp the country. The shares of the 12 independent regional Federal Reserve banks will be owned by its member banks which are all Rothchilds owned banks. The shares of the Federal Reserve Bank will be owned by a group of undisclosed investors with vast resources to supply the necessary gold reserve. The central FED reserve bank will be administered by a committee selected by the subordinate FED banks. The president of the USA will select a chairman from a list prepared by the central FED bank and appoint him. The sub-FEDs will be governed by committees selected by the member banks.
.
.
.

A list of the primary shareholders in the Federal Reserve Bank was accidentally released by FED in 1990's. They are:

1) The Rothschild Family - London
2) The Rothschild Family - Berlin
3) The Lazard Brothers - Paris
4) Israel Seiff - Italy
5) Kuhn-Loeb Company - Germany
6) The Warburgs - Amsterdam
7) The Warburgs - Hamburg
8) Lehman Brothers - New York
9) Goldman & Sachs - New York
10) The Rockefeller Family - New York

All of them are Rothchild family members or in-laws or Rothschild front organizations. For example Rockefeller family of New York is supposed to be American Christian family but in reality it is a Jewish family connected to Rothchilds by marriage. These are the families which would later finance the Russian communist revolution which overthrew Czar's Royal family.

Paul Warburg in his book 'The Federal Reserve System: Its Origin and Growth' explains in many words that the conspirators met in secrecy because there was widespread suspicion of Jewish Bankers and the Wall Street and their power and ambitions.
The conspiring Rothchilds Bankers funded and staffed Woodrow Wilson's campaign for President. They also funded and staffed election campaigns of several senators and congressmen. Woodrow Wilson and these senators and congressmen had committed to passing the Federal Reserve Bank Act.

Senator Aldrich, introduced the bill to create Federal Reserve Bank in congress. The bankers opposed the bill saying that it is anti-banking and intended to destroy the Jewish monopoly in banking. This fake opposition was intended to mislead the public. The bill did not pass. Majority of the congressmen and senators had left

Washington and went home by train for Christmas holidays. The senators and congressmen who were elected into office with the help of the Bankers' money and support by Newspapers owned by Bankers, stayed behind. This bi-partisan group of crooked congressmen and senators introduced the Federal Reserve Bank bill after striking the name of Senator Aldrich from it. There were not enough congressmen and senators to satisfy the quorum. They introduced and passed the bill without the quorum in both congress and senate within minutes and then sent it to the president for his signature. Within 15 minutes of passing the bill, President Woodrow Wilson who was contractually obligated to the bankers to sign it, signed the bill and made it law and the Federal Reserve Bank came into existence. Before majority of the congressmen reached their homes by train, Federal Reserve bank notes were circulating in their cities.

Before the Bill was introduced in congress, the conspirators had already registered the FED as a private corporation. Registration of one corporation did not catch any reporter's eyes. There were approximately 300 people or banks that became stockholders in the Federal Reserve Banking System, each purchasing stock at $100 per share. It seems every member of the Rothschild family got one share in the FED. This stock is not publicly traded. The FED never held any gold or silver reserve of any kind. FED had very little expense because it does not cost much money to print bank notes, which is the only product of this corporation. Before the bill was introduced in Congress, they had already printed enough paper money and stockpiled in each city ready to be circulated.

The FED banking system collects hundreds of billions of dollars in interest annually and distributes the profits to its shareholders. In the years that followed, every shareholder of FED must have received hundreds of billions of dollars in dividend for their $100 share. The Congress illegally gave the FED the right to print money. The FED creates money from nothing, and loans it back to the people through banks, and charges interest on people's currency.

The FED buys Government debt (bonds) with money printed on paper and charges U.S. taxpayers' interest. This is fraud.

Some of the secret shareholders of the Central and regional FEDs have been accidentally revealed. They are:

First National Bank of New York
James Stillman National City Bank, New York
Mary W. Harnman
National Bank of Commerce, New York
A.D. Jiullard
Hanover National Bank, New York
Jacob Schiff
Chase National Bank, New York
Thomas F. Ryan
Paul Warburg
William Rockefeller
Levi P. Morton
M.T. Pyne
George F. Baker
Percy Pyne
Mrs. G.F. St. George
J.W. Sterling
Katherine St. George
H.P. Davidson
J.P. Morgan (Equitable Life/Mutual Life)
Edith Brevour T. Baker

The banks finance the election campaigns of sympathetic candidates. Usually better funded candidates win. Banks also employ members of the Congress on weekends with lucrative salaries. Additionally, the Banks have bought up Newspapers, Radio stations, TV stations, book and magazine publishers and Movie Studios. With their money, banks decide who gets elected and what policies they will follow.

Presidents Lincoln, Jackson, and Kennedy tried to stop this family of bankers by printing U.S. dollars without charging the taxpayers interest. Today, if the government runs a deficit, the FED prints dollars through the U.S. Treasury, buys the debt, and the dollars are circulated into the economy. In 2015, the FED made a profit of almost a trillion dollars. This is the interest on the money they printed virtually cost free. Close to 80% of the personal federal income taxes went to pay this interest. Nobody has ever audited the FED's books.

Rep. McFadden: "The FEDs are private credit monopolies which prey upon the people of the United States for the benefit of themselves and their foreign customers, foreign and domestic speculators and swindlers, and the rich and predatory money lenders. This is an era of economic misery and the Federal Reserve Board and the Federal Reserve banks are fully liable for causing that misery... Every effort has been made by the Federal Reserve Board to conceal its power but the truth is the Federal Reserve Board has usurped the government of the United States. It controls everything here and it controls all our foreign relations. It makes and breaks governments at will. ... No man and no body of men is more entrenched in power than the arrogant credit monopoly which operates the Federal Reserve Board and the Federal Reserve banks. These evil-doers have robbed this country of more than enough money to pay the national debt many times over."

In July 1968, Rockefeller, through Chase Manhattan Bank, controlled 5.9% of the stock in CBS. Also, the bank had gained interlocking directorates with ABC. In 1974, Chase Manhattan Bank's stake in CBS rose to 14.1% and NBC to 4.5%. Chase Manhattan Bank obtained 6.7% of ABC, and held stock in 28 broadcasting firms. Chase Manhattan Bank is only one of 300 shareholders of the FED. It is believed other FED owners have similar holdings in the media. To control the media, FED bankers call in their loans if the media disagrees with them.

Rockefeller also controls the Council on Foreign Relations (CFR), the sole purpose of which is to control foreign policy of the government and to create a 'world government'. The CFR controls many major newspapers and magazines and most of the newscasters are members. Most corporations in USA are owned by FED shareholders.

According to the Congressional record, U.S. Government can buy back the FED at any time for $450 million. If they do, the U.S. Treasury could collect all the profit instead of the 300 original shareholders of the FED. $22.4 trillion of U.S. debt could be exchanged for non- interest bearing currency. There would be no inflation because there would be no additional currency in circulation. Lincoln and Kennedy have shown the way.

The real solution to the money problem is to print money the way the Constitution requires, not the new proposed international money. By printing its own money, America will keep its sovereignty and economic prosperity.

Then why doesn't the Congress do it? If a Congressman tries to change the system, the banks will fund a campaign to recall him and fund the election campaign of his opponent in the next election. Look what happened to the speaker of the house Eric Cantor. The new Congressman will obviously support the FED. When Congressmen retire, their political campaign funds are theirs to keep tax free. Congressmen can receive huge campaign contributions and they can retire very rich by doing what the Bankers tell them. Profits of FED and the dividends paid out by the FED are not taxed either.

Rothchild bankers funded both sides of all European wars since 1762 and also French revolution, Russian Revolution, WWI and WWII. They created fake colonial money to destroy the Americans during the Revolutionary War. They tried to finance both sides in the American Civil War. Abraham Lincoln refused and the South accepted. They financed both sides with money printed on paper and earned enormous profits in real gold and silver. They created every American depression and profited greatly from it all. More wars create more debt which means more profit to the bankers. They created the false-flag event on 9/11 in NY and instigated the endless wars in the Middle East. It is estimated to have cost America 6 trillion dollars which was borrowed from FED on interest.

According to congressional records, the bankers buy stocks, create inflation, sell their stocks before the market crashes, then buy up stocks at cheaper prices. This is illegal but who would dare prosecute big campaign contributors. Thomas Jefferson predicted this would happen if a private bank is allowed to create money. Thomas Jefferson: "I believe that banking institutions are more dangerous to our liberties than standing armies.... Already they have raised up a money aristocracy that has set the government at defiance. The issuing power of money should be taken from the banks and restored to the people to whom it properly belongs." The American Revolution was a struggle to wrest control of wealth from the Bank of England and to restore the centers of power to the People. The Constitution is specific about the authority of the People to control their money.

Ben Franklin: 'the inability of the colonists to get the power to issue their own money permanently out of the hands of George III and the international bankers was the prime reason for the Revolutionary War.'

Thomas Jefferson: "If the American people ever allow private banks to control the issue of currency, first by inflation, then by deflation, the banks and corporations that will grow up around them will deprive the people of all property until their children will wake up homeless on the continent their fathers conquered."

Napoleon: "When a government is dependent upon bankers for money, they and not the leaders of the government control the situation, since the hand that gives is above the hand that takes... Money has no motherland; financiers are without patriotism and without decency; their sole object is gain."

In 1879 the Supreme Court declared that the U.S. Government can legally issue United States Notes, debt-free and interest-free.

11. The Rothschilds

Nobody has seen air but we know there is air because we breathe it. Rothschild is like that. Nobody knows who or what it is but everybody is affected by him/it. Rothschild owns almost everything in this world. He is wealthier than Kubera, the Hindu god of wealth. 75% of all the wealth in this universe is owned by Rothschilds. Unlike Kubera, Rothschild can create money and wealth out of nothing. There is no limit to how much money he can create. He owns 90% of all the gold ever mined on this earth and controls the gold and diamond trade of this world. At his wink empires fall and he can create new world-powers with a word from his mouth. He can lunch 50,000 nuclear bombs at the flick of his small finger. He is definitely more powerful than God!

Around 1000 AD, Mongol nomads of Khazaria, in the steppes of Kazakhstan, were nature-worshippers, like most Asian tribes in those days. Suddenly, they faced an existential threat. Christian Russians on the north wanted to overthrow them because they were pagans (nature-worshippers). The Muslims on the south wanted to do the same for the same reason. To save their community, the king and citizens of Khazaria decided to stay neutral by converting to Pharisaic Judaism, which was the most vicious and ruthless Talmud-based Judaism. But, King of Russia attacked and sacked them. Some citizens escaped to Poland. Over a period of time, they spread to other parts of Eastern Europe and to Western Europe. They lived in their own ghetto enclaves and they engaged in nefarious activities which Christians of Europe wouldn't do. They made their living by stealing, trading, crooked scams, gold jewelry, usury, prostitution, murder, etc. These immoral and illegal and criminal activities and thuggery made a lot of money for them. They learned early on to stick together to succeed as gangsters. The difference between Gypsies and Jews is that the Jews learned their Holy book (Talmud) and were therefore literate and they were ruthless and murdered their way through the host society while Gypsies shunned book-learning and stayed as nomads and were passive without any ambition.

Some of these Khazar Jews moved to Germany. They took German names and dressed like Germans to hide their Khazar nomadic identity. They spoke a strange dialect called Yiddish which is a mixture of their native Khazari language, German and Hebrew. Very similar to Hinglish (mixture of Hindi and English) spoken by many Hindus in London. The host population did not understand what they were talking among themselves while they understood what the local population was talking. This was great advantage for their nefarious criminal activities.

Christians say these are the Satanic people Bible talks about in Rev. 2: 9, "I know the blasphemy of them which say they are Jews, and are not, but are the synagogue of Satan." (interpretation: You claim to be Jews, but you are not Jews; you are children of Devil.)

One of the goldsmiths and usurer named Moses Amschel Bauer made lots of money through money lending and by working as a coin counter. In those days money counting was a recognized profession. To catch the attention of potential customers, Moses hung a red-colored hexagonal shield above his door. The hexagon has six sides and six points and six triangles. It has some hidden meaning like 666, which is the number of Satan according to Christian Bible.

His son Mayer Amschel Bauer worked for Oppenheimer, a Jewish banker. He was successful and became a partner in the bank. There he became acquainted with General von Estorff.
When his father died, Mayer took over his father's business. He noticed that the red sign caught the attention of many a customers. So he decided to add 'red sign' to his name. In German, red sign is 'Rot Schild'. In English this is pronounced and written as 'Rothchild'. Two hundred years later, his descendant obtained some land in Palestine through murders, terrorism, and ethnic

cleansing and established Israel and put this hexagon on its flag to show that the country is owned by Rothchild.

Mayer Amschel Rothschild, found out that General von Estorff works for the court of Prince William IX of Hesse-Hanau, the richest royal house in Europe. He made friendship with General von Estorff in the guise of selling him some coins and trinkets at discounted price. It was a ploy to get noticed by flashy Prince William. He offered Prince William valuable gold coins at discount price. Prince was interested. He bought some coins and also directed some others to his business. He discovered that loaning money to royalty and governments is very profitable. The amounts are large and the loans are guaranteed by taxes. In 1769, Mayer Amschel Rothschild got permission to use the title 'merchant to Prince William of Hanau'. This title gave him respectability and acceptance in the community and boosted his business.

In those days, there were several gangs, in every city. Some of the groups operated in secrecy for their own protection and they called themselves secret societies. Freemasons gangs were popular. A wicked Jew named Adam Weishaupt converted to Catholicism and joined the 'Order of Jesuits'. Jesuits had a system to keep their special knowledge secret. Jesuits were organized in concentric layers. The outer layer had no special knowledge. Those who did well in the outer layer were promoted to inner layers. The secret knowledge was revealed to those in the innermost group only. After learning their modus operandi, Adam Weishaupt left the Catholic Church to make his own secret society.

At that time Mayer Amschel Rothschild befriended Adam Weishaupt and asked him to make a secret society to rule the world based on Talmud. Talmud teaches that only Jews are humans and that they are created specially to rule the world and that they are supposed to defeat, subjugate and enslave the whole world and that non-Jews are not humans and are filthy animals and they should be treated as such and that their property belong to Jews. Adam Weishaupt laid plans for destroying the non-Jews and then ruling the world based on Talmud. If anybody knew about his plans, they would have killed him and his devilish plans. So, he had to operate through secret societies, revealing the whole plan only to trusted members in the innermost circle.

The good thing about secret societies is that everything is compartmentalized. Nobody knows more than what they are told and nobody is told everything. Mayer Amschel Rothschild was making enough money through usury, money lending to royalty and fractional banking (fraudulent banking). He could afford to set up and finance a secret society. He called his secret society 'the Illuminati' which means those who have the light of the morning star. Jesuits worshipped Jesus and Illuminati worshipped Morning Star also known as Lucifer/Satan/Devil. The organization was completed on May 1 of 1776 and that is why May 1 is considered a big birth-day celebration for the Illuminati. Rothchilds funded the communist revolution and established communism in Russia. 1st of May was made a big holiday for Soviet Union to show that conquest of Russia, the largest Christian country of the time, was one of the fruits of the 'Illuminati' plan started on May 1, 1776. When Rothchilds got complete control of the US Monetary system, they put Freemason / illuminati symbol on the US one dollar bill. In that symbol 1776 is prominently displayed to show that American money is one of the fruits of Rothschild's plan that started in 1776.

All the Jews of the world together could not militarily defeat the large community of non-Jews in a frontal assault. Even the British technique of divide and conquer won't work because non-Jews are numerous. To cut a diamond you have to use a diamond. Adam Weishaupt devised a plan to cut the non-Jewish community into pieces and then pit them against each other and grind them to powder. He planned to divide the non-Jews (Talmud calls them Goym) into two or more political, economic, social, and religious groups and make the groups fight each other. All sides would be armed and financed by Rothchilds and then false-flag incidents would be provided in order for them to fight each other. They would be made to destroy national governments, religious institutions and each other.

Dr. Eric T. Karlstrom wrote in 2006 in 'Techniques and Strategies of the New World Order': "Amschel Mayer Rothschild, Jewish international banker, allegedly, gave a speech to other wealthy individuals in Frankfurt, Germany in 1773. In this speech, he outlined this program for eventual world domination by an oligarchy of the wealthy:

1) Since men are inclined more toward evil than good, they can be governed best by using violence and terrorism rather than discussion and persuasion.

2) Since political freedom is an idea rather than a fact, it is only necessary to preach liberalism and the people will surrender their freedom to central government for an idea. This power is then to be seized.

3) The power of gold (money) can overcome the power of liberal leaders. It doesn't matter who will be used to destroy existing governments because whoever does so will need money, and that is entirely in our hands.

4) The use of any means to achieve our goal is justified (the ends justify the means).

5) Our right lies in force (might makes right).

6) We will use alcohol, drugs, and moral corruption of all kinds to corrupt the youth.

7) Our policy will be to cause wars and then direct peace conferences in such a manner that neither side obtains territorial gains.

8) The power of our sources must remain secret.

9) Our wealth should be used to subsidize candidates elected to office who will pass laws favorable to our enterprises. Politicians will be controlled by our behind the scenes "experts", "specialists", "advisors", and "agentur".

10) We will use criminals and subversives to create violence and terror among the masses. After these groups have done their damage, our agents will appear on the scene to exterminate them, thus appearing to be saviors of the oppressed.

11) We will use our combined wealth to control the press and other outlets of public information and use them to spread propaganda and lies while we remain hidden in the background clear of blame.

12) We will use high sounding phrases and make lavish promises. Afterward, the opposite can be given.

13) We will bring about industrial depressions and financial panics to create unemployment and hunger.

14) By controlling the mobs, we can eliminate any opposition that stands in our way.

15) We will infiltrate Continental Free Masonry and organize a secret society within a secret society. And we will use Lodges of the Grand Orient to spread propaganda.

16) Our goal will be world government.

17) We will create economic war through higher and higher taxes and by subsidizing special interest minority groups. By stimulating greed amongst the masses, the masses themselves will help destroy their own economy and themselves. Matters will be arranged so that increased wages and salaries will bring about no real benefit.

18) We will build up arms between the major powers, and then provoke an incident and force them into war so they will destroy each other's governments and religious institutions.

19) We will infiltrate our agents into all classes of people, in schools and elsewhere to corrupt the youth by teaching them theories and principles we know to be false.

20) We will substitute international arbitration for law."

Weishaupt soon infiltrated the Continental Order of Freemasons with this Illuminati doctrine and established lodges of the Grand Orient to be their secret headquarters. Mayer Amschel Rothschild financed all this. The Freemasonry concept and Masonic Lodges flourish worldwide even today.

Weishaupt also recruited 2,000 paid followers including the most intelligent men in the field of arts and literature, education, science, finance, and industry. They were instructed to follow the following Freemason methods to control people:

1. Use monetary and sex bribery to obtain control of men already in high places, in the various levels of all governments and other fields of endeavor. Once influential persons had fallen for the lies, deceits, and temptations of the Illuminati they were to be held in bondage by application of political and other forms of blackmail, threats of financial ruin, public exposure, and fiscal harm, even death to themselves and loved members of their families. The Monica Lewinski scandal involving President Bill Clinton is a good example. After that incident, Illuminati could force Bill Clinton to declare war in Bosnia and kill millions and destroy the last socialist country in Europe, and remove all the guards put in place after 1928 stock market crash to prevent another like it and sign NAFTA the north American trade Union agreement which was a step towards achieving the one world government which Rothchilds are striving for.

2) The faculties of colleges and universities were to cultivate students possessing exceptional mental ability belonging to well-bred families with international leanings, and recommend them for special training in internationalism, or rather the notion that only a one- world government can put an end to recurring wars and strife. Such training was to be provided by granting scholarships to those selected by the Illuminati. People like Bill Clinton are examples of such education. Rhode Scholarships are meant for developing and training talented people to achieve the goals of Rothchilds.

3) All influential people trapped into coming under the control of the Illuminati, plus the students who had been specially educated and trained, were to be used as agents and placed behind the scenes of all governments as experts and specialists. This was so they would advise the top executives to adopt policies which would in the long-run serve the secret plans of the Illuminati one-world conspiracy and bring about the destruction of the governments and religions they were elected or appointed to serve. The behind the scenes experts remain in place while the face of the administration changes. For example, the policies of destroying communism and the Muslim world started by George Bush senior continued unabated through the period of Bill Clinton who was a pacifist and through George Bush Jr. and through President Barack Obama who came in with declared aim to end war but instead ended up starting more wars and killing more millions than his predecessors.

4) To obtain absolute-control of the press, so that all news and information could be slanted in order to make the masses believe that a one-world government is the only solution to our many and varied problems. At that time the only mass-communications media was the press. Now we have radio and television and internet and illuminati owns all the media – including Twitter, Face Book, Google and Microsoft, TV, Newspapers, Radio and printed

books and publications (Amazon) - in the modern world. Now it is possible for Rothchilds to make the whole world believe it is necessary to abandon the national currencies and accept a world currency.

Even though according to official Jewish source, the Jewish Almanac, there were 3.5 million Jews before WWII and there were 3.75 million after it, they have made the whole world believe that 6 million Jews were killed by Nazi Germany.

Even though it is impossible for a bullet to take several 90 degree turns and hit a target from multiple angles, the word was made to believe President Kennedy was killed by a lone assassin with a magic bullet.

Even though it is contrary to common sense and to laws of physics, they made the whole world believe that 19 fumbling Arab idiots took over four airplanes with box cutters and precision-hit two tall buildings (Bldg. #1 and #2) and those two buildings plus another one little farther away (Bldg.#7) exploded into powder and neatly fell into their footprints as in controlled demolition. This was in accordance with the Rothchild/Freemason agenda to provide the incidents to make two groups fight. America was told by the media that the countries that did not have Rothchild owned central banks (Afghanistan, Iraq, Syria, Libya, Iran, North Korea and Cuba) were responsible for the controlled demolition of the buildings in NY. Then, America destroyed Iraq, Afghanistan, Libya and Syria.

In 1784, Rothchild ordered the French Revolution. Detailed instructions were sent to Maximilien Robespierre. The courier from Frankfurt to Paris was hit by lightning and the detailed plans were discovered by Bavarian authorities. In 1785, Bavarian government outlawed the Illuminati and closed all the Bavarian lodges of the Grand Orient. In 1786, Bavarian government sent 'The Original Writings of The Order and Sect of The Illuminati' to heads of churches and governments of Europe. But the warnings were ignored. Human beings ignored the warnings of Noah before flood and they ignored warnings of Jesus about the coming destruction of Jerusalem and even about the end of days. How can people be expected to believe the warnings about a secret group? Consequently the French revolution was started as planned in 1789 and continued until 1793, until all the goals of the revolution have been achieved. Destruction of the power of Catholic Church was one of the goals.

In 1790, Mayer Amschel Rothschild stated: "Let me issue and control a nation's money and I care not who sits in the throne." The following year, Rothschild's agent Alexander Hamilton set up a central bank in the USA called the First Bank of the United States and Rothchild got 'control of America's money'.

In 1798, Professor John Robison, a high degree mason in the Scottish Rite of Freemasonry, and confidant of Adam Weishaupt, published "Proofs of a Conspiracy Against All the Religions and Governments of Europe Carried on in the Secret Meetings of Freemasons, Illuminati and Reading Societies." But the warnings were ignored by all governments because those governments were advised by Freemason experts behind the scenes. In 1798, Nathan Mayer Rothschild set up a banking house in London.

In 1806, Rothchild financially supported Napoleon and encouraged him to make war with Europe. Napoleon declared his intention to sack Prince William IX of Hesse-Hanau. Prince William fled to Denmark, after entrusting his fortune of $3,000,000 with Mayer Amschel Rothschild for safekeeping. According to the Jewish Encyclopedia, 1905 edition, Volume 10, page 494: '.. this money was hidden away in wine casks, and, escaped the search of Napoleon's soldiers when they entered Frankfurt." The money was never returned by Rothschild to Prince William IX of Hesse-Hanau. The encyclopedia states: "Nathan Mayer Rothschild invested this $3,000,000 in, gold from the East India Company knowing that it would be needed for Wellington's peninsula campaign." On the stolen money Nathan made, "no less than four profits: i) On the sale of Wellington's paper which he bought at 50 cents on the dollar and collected at par; ii) on the sale of gold to Wellington; iii) on its repurchase; and iv) on forwarding it to Portugal." Thus, crooked Mayer Rothchild made a fortune. And Rothchild set up a central bank in Vienna, Austria.

In 1811, US congress refused to renew the charter of Rothchild central bank. Nathan Mayer Rothschild threatened: "Either the application for renewal of the charter is granted, or the United States will find itself involved in a most disastrous war." United States stood firm. Nathan Mayer Rothschild ordered British Government: 'Teach those impudent Americans a lesson. Bring them back to colonial status." In 1812, British declared war on the United States. The Rothschild's plan was to cause the United States to borrow large amount of money for the war and go into deep debt to Rothchild bank (the only bank in town) and be forced to renew the charter for Rothschild's First Bank of the United States. In that year, Mayer Amschel Rothschild died. In his will he laid out specific rules for the House of Rothschild. 'All key positions in the family business were only to be held by male family members, including five sons and one bastard son.' He had five daughters. Children of daughters are considered part of the family in accordance with Talmudic laws.

If Mayer had 11 children and each of them had similar number of children in each generation and 20 years is considered one generation, that would mean in 250 years there would be millions of Zionist descendants to Mayer Rothchild by 2016. Fortunately, he had set up a system to own all the wealth of the world and all his descendants will be billionaires until end of world.

The will required that: 'No public inventory of his estate was to be published; no legal action was to be taken with regard to the value of the inheritance; the eldest son of the eldest son was to become the head of the family.' As laid out in the will, Nathan Mayer

Rothschild became head of the family.
That year, Jacob (James) Mayer Rothschild set up a central bank in Paris, France.

In 1815, the five Rothschild brothers worked together to supply gold to both Wellington's army and Napoleon's army, and thus began their policy of funding both sides in wars. The Rothschilds instigated wars because wars are massive generators of risk-free debt. This is because they are guaranteed by the government of a country, and therefore the people of the country would pay. Also, it doesn't matter who loses or wins, because the loans are given on the guarantee that the winner will honor the debts of the defeated.

Rothschilds set up postal service network of secret routes and fast couriers. Rothschild couriers were the only merchants allowed to pass through the English and French blockades. Through their couriers, they always knew the current events ahead of anybody else.

When the Battle of Waterloo was won by the British, Rothschild received the news from his courier a full 24 hours before Wellington's own courier. At that time British bonds called consuls were traded on the floor of the stock exchange. Nathan Mayer Rothschild instructed all his workers on the floor to start selling consuls. Other traders, who knew Rothchilds get his news ahead of time, believed that the British had lost the war. So they started selling their consuls. The value of the consuls plummeted. At that time, Nathan Mayer Rothschild secretly instructed his workers to purchase all the consuls they could lay their hands on.
When news came through that the British had actually won the war, the consuls went up to a level even higher than before leaving Nathan Mayer Rothschild with a return of approximately 20 to 1 on his investment. This gave the Rothschild family complete control of the British economy. Following Napoleon's defeat, England became the financial center of the world. Nathan Mayer

Rothschild's 'Bank of England' (BoE) was the central bank of British Empire.

In 1815, Nathan Mayer Rothschild said: "I care not what puppet is placed upon the throne of England to rule the Empire on which the sun never sets. The man who controls Britain's money supply controls the British Empire, and I control the British money supply." He bragged that in the 17 years he had been in England he had increased the £20,000 stake given to him by his father, 2500 times to £50 million. By 1890, Rothschild family controlled half the wealth of the world.

Most of the European governments were in debt to the Rothschilds, and had no choice but to give in to Rothschild's wishes. Rothchild wanted to realize his dream of 'one world government' which will give him complete control and subjugation of the civilized world, which Talmud says he is entitled to have. To make that happen, he convened the Congress of Vienna, which started in September of 1814 and concluded in June of 1815. 'Tsar Alexander I' of Russia, who had not succumbed to a Rothschild central bank, would not go along with the plan of one world government under Rothchild and the plan failed. Furious Nathan Mayer Rothschild swore that one day he or his descendants would destroy the Tsar Alexander I's entire family and descendants. 102 years later, after Rothschild-funded-Bolsheviks took control of Russia, the entire family of the Czar was murdered, on orders from Rothchilds.

In 1816, after the deaths of thousands of American and British soldiers, the American Congress gave in to Rothchilds and passed a bill giving control of American Money Supply to Rothschild's central bank called the Second Bank of the United States, for 20 years. Then Rothchild called off the war.

After their disastrous defeat at Waterloo in 1817, French Government took massive loans to rebuild the country by issuing vast amounts of bonds. Rothchild bought most of these bonds causing their value to increase. On November 5th 1818, Rothchilds dumped the bonds on the open market causing their value to plummet and France went into a financial panic. The Rothschilds then stepped in to take control of the French money supply. Similar tricks were played by Rothchild banks in USA in 1907 causing the banking panic that eventually paved the way for creation of the FED in 1913.

In 1821, Kalmann (Carl) Mayer Rothschild was sent to Naples, Italy, to do business with the Vatican. Later, Pope Gregory XVI conferred upon him the 'Order of St. George'. In those days, everybody kissed the toe of the Pope when they met him. But, when Kalmann comes in, Pope would shake his hands instead. Pope would have kissed the toe of Kalmann if he was asked. In 1823, the Rothschilds took over the worldwide financial operations of the Catholic Church. From that powerful position, Rothchilds started destroying the Catholic Church financially and made it totally dependent on Rothchilds. From 1958 onwards all Popes have been Illuminati members and secret (crypto) Jews.

Rothchild wanted to defang the doctrines of Catholic Church and Pope John XXIII complied and convened the Second Vatican Council (October 1962 - December 1965). Vatican II changed all traditional beliefs of Catholic Church and denounced the belief that Jews killed Jesus as described in Bible. Catholic Church acknowledged that Jews are God's special selected people and they will go to heaven without believing in Jesus. Rothschild's bank ruined the finances of Vatican. Vatican became deep in debt to Rothchild and Pope had to lick the boots of Rothchilds to meet payroll.

In 1822, the emperor of Austria made the five Rothschild brothers Barons. In 1833, President Andrew Jackson shifted government's deposits from Rothschild's Second Bank of the United States to non-Jewish banks. Rothschilds were furious, and they contracted the money supply and it caused a depression. President Jackson said: "You are a den of thieves, vipers, and I intend to rout you out, and by the Eternal God, I will rout you out." On January 30, 1835, an assassin sent by Rothchild shot at President Jackson, but both his pistols misfired. The assassin, Richard Lawrence, who was found not guilty by reason of insanity, later bragged that powerful people in Europe had hired him and promised to protect him if he were caught. In 1836, President Andrew Jackson refused to renew the Rothchild bank's charter. Rothchilds kept trying and in 1913, they were successful again.

In 1836, the Rothschilds acquired the rights in the Almadén quicksilver mines in Spain. Quicksilver is a vital component in the refining of gold and silver and thus, Rothschilds got a world-monopoly on Gold and silver.

In 1840, the Rothschilds became the Bank of England's bullion brokers and they set up agencies in California and Australia. In 1844, Rothschilds purchased the United Coal Mines, the world's largest industrial concern in Europe.

In 1836, Rothschilds won lucrative contracts to build continental railway lines in America and in Europe.

In 1848, Rothchild ordered and funded Karl Marx, a Khazari (Ashkenazi) Jew, to write and publish "The Communist Manifesto." Rothschilds also ordered and funded Karl Ritter of Frankfurt University to write and publish the anti-thesis to communism. Friedrich Wilhelm Nietzsche was ordered and funded to develop "Nietzscheanism" based on Karl Ritter's ideas. Nietzecheanism was later developed into Fascism and then into Nazism. Rothchild used Nazism to foment WWI and WWII.

Rothschilds ordered and funded Marx, Ritter, and Nietzsche because the illuminati principle says, opposing ideologies should be used to divide human race into opposing camps so that they could be armed and then brainwashed into fighting and destroying each other, and particularly, to destroy all political and religious institutions. This was the plan devised by Weishaupt in 1776.

In 1849, Gutle Schnaper, wife of Mayer Amschel Rothschild, said: "If my sons did not want wars, there would be none."

In an effort to force the United States to accept a central bank, Rothchild instigated the American civil war. The British and French were supporting the south. The south accepted funding from Rothchilds for the war. In 1861, Rothchilds offered President Abraham Lincoln war funding at 36% interest. Abraham Lincoln refused and printed his own debt-free money called 'greenbacks' and informed the public that this is now legal tender for both public and private debts. With greenbacks, he won the war. Lincoln said: "We gave the people of this republic the greatest blessing they ever had - their own paper money to pay their own debts."

The Times of London wrote: "If that mischievous financial policy, which had its origin in the North American Republic, should become indurated down to a fixture, then that government will furnish its own money without cost. It will pay off debts and be without a debt. It will have all the money necessary to carry on its commerce. It will become prosperous beyond precedent in the history of civilized governments of the world. The brains and the wealth of all countries will go to North America. That government must be destroyed or it will destroy every monarchy on the globe."

The Tsar of Russia, Alexander II refused the attempts of Rothchilds to set up a central bank in Russia. When he found out that the Rothschilds were going to destroy America, he warned that if either England or France actively intervened in the American Civil War, and helped the South, Russia would consider it a declaration of war. He also sent part of his Pacific Fleet to port in San Francisco and another part to New York.

John D. Rockefeller, a member of the Rothschild family, formed an oil business called Standard Oil and took over all the competition. In 1864: Rothschild, August Belmont, the Democratic Party's National Chairman, nominated General George McClellan to run against President Abraham Lincoln. He lost. Belmont was furious and decided to take revenge. President Abraham Lincoln said: "I have two great enemies, the Southern Army in front of me, and the financial institutions in the rear. Of the two, the one in my rear is my greatest foe." On orders of August Belmont Rothchild, a conspiracy was hatched and President Lincoln was assassinated on April 14, two months before the end of the American Civil War.

Jacob Schiff, a Rothschild, was sent to America at the age of 18, with instructions to:
1. Gain control of America's money system through the establishment of a central bank.
2. Find desirable men, who for a price, would be willing to serve as stooges for the Illuminati and promote them into high places in the Federal government, the Congress, Supreme Court, and all the Federal agencies.
3. Create minority group strife throughout the nations, particularly targeting the whites and blacks.
4. Create a movement to destroy religion, especially Christianity, in the United States.

An American General named Albert Pike, was enticed into the Illuminati by Giuseppe Mazzini. Pike was elected Sovereign Grand Commander of the Scottish Rite of Freemasonry's Southern Jurisdiction in 1859. He became the most powerful Freemason in America. He would retain that post for 32 years until his death in 1891. In 1872, he published the book "Morals and Dogma of the Ancient and Accepted Scottish Rite of Freemasonry" in which he stated: 'Lucifer, the Light-bearer! Strange and mysterious name to give to the Spirit of Darkness! Lucifer, the Son of the Morning! Is it he who bears the Light, and with its splendors intolerable blinds feeble, sensual or selfish Souls? Doubt it not!'. In 1871, Pike completed his famous military blueprint for three world wars and various revolutions throughout the world, culminating in the establishment of one world government ruled by Rothchilds.

See 'the three world wars' on page: 94

The WWI is to be fought for the purpose of destroying the Tsar in Russia, as promised by Nathan Mayer Rothschild in 1815. The Tsar is to be replaced with communism which is to be used to attack religions, predominantly Christianity. The differences between the British and German empires are to be used to foment this war.

The WWII is to be used to foment the controversy between fascism and political Zionism with the slaughter of Jews in Germany, which will bring hatred against the German people. This is designed to destroy fascism (which the Rothschilds created) and increase the power of political Zionism (establishment of sovereign criminal nation called Israel). This war is also designed to increase the power of communism to the same level as united Christendom.

The WWIII is to be played out by stirring up hatred of the Muslim world for the purposes of pitting the Islamic world against the political Zionists. While this is going on, the remaining nations would be forced to fight themselves into a state of mental, physical, spiritual and economic exhaustion.

On August 15th of 1871, Albert Pike wrote a letter (at the present time, it is catalogued in the British Museum) to Giuseppe Mazzini in which he described the planned 'three World Wars' leading to creation of 'one world government' under the rule of Rothchild.

Rothschilds financed the revolutionary activities of Guiseppe Mazzini and his successor Adrian Lemmy, and Lemmy's successors Lenin and Trotsky, and Lenin's successor Stalin.

In 1873 Rothchilds purchased Rio Tinto copper mines in Spain, and got a monopoly in copper, an essential component in war production.

In 1875, Jacob Schiff, financed other Rothchild family members John D. Rockefeller, Edward R. Harriman and Andrew Carnegie to create oil monopoly called 'Standard Oil Company', to create railroad empire, and to create steel empire respectively. And they established monopolies in American business.

Rothchilds purchased the controlling shares of Suez Canal and monopolized the movement of merchant and navy ships through that area.

In 1876, Otto von Bismarck stated: "The division of the United States into two federations of equal force was decided long before the civil war by the Rothchilds. They were afraid that the United States, if it remained in one block and as one nation, would attain economical and financial independence, which would upset Rothschild's financial domination over the world. The Rothschilds foresaw the tremendous booty if they could replace one vigorous, confident and self-providing Republic with two feeble democracies indebted to the financiers. Therefore they started their emissaries in order to exploit the question of slavery and thus dig an abyss between the two parts of the Republic."

In 1880, Rothschild's agents began fermenting a series of pogroms predominantly in Russia, but also in Poland, Bulgaria and Romania. These pogroms were initiated for the purpose of creating a large Jewish base in America, who when they arrived, would be educated to register as Democrat voters. These pogroms resulted in the slaughter of thousands of innocent Jews, causing approximately 2 million to flee, mainly to New York, but also to Chicago, Philadelphia, Boston and Los Angeles. Some twenty years later, this would result in a massive Democratic power base in the United States. They would be used to elect Rothschild front-men such as Woodrow Wilson to the Presidency to carry out the bidding of the Rothschilds.

In 1881, President James A. Garfield said: "Whoever controls the volume of money in our country is absolute master of all industry and commerce and when you realize that the entire system is very easily controlled one way or another by a few powerful men at the top, you will not have to be told how periods of inflation and depression originate." Two weeks later he was assassinated by agents of Rothchilds.

In 1886, Rothschilds bought up Russia's oil fields and established the 'Caspian and Black Sea Petroleum Company' and it became second largest oil producer in the world. Later the name was changed to 'Royal Dutch Shell Oil Company'.

Rothchilds controlled the illegal opium trafficking in China. In 1887, they bought up 'Kimberley diamond mines' and 'De Beers' in South Africa and mines in India and established the diamond and gold monopoly.

In 1891, an anonymous British labor leader wrote: "This blood-sucking crew *(Rothchilds)* has been the cause of untold mischief and misery in Europe during the present century, and has piled up its prodigious wealth chiefly through fomenting wars between States which ought never to have quarreled. Whenever there is trouble in Europe, wherever rumors of war circulate and men's minds are distraught with fear of change and calamity you may be sure that a hook-nosed Rothschild is at his games somewhere near the region of the disturbance." Rothchild was disturbed by this comment. To stop such comments in the press, Rothchilds purchased the news reporting agencies 'Reuters' in London, 'Havas' in France, and 'Wolf' in Germany and all other news wire agencies in existence in Europe. And Rothchilds were never mentioned in any news stories afterwards.

In 1895, Edmond James de Rothschild visited Palestine and funded first Jewish colonies there to create a Rothschild owned sovereign country, to be used as a basis for Rothschild's worldwide criminal activities.

In 1897, Rothschilds founded the Zionist Congress to promote Zionism. Its goal is to assemble all Jews into Rothchild-owned country 'Israel'. Theodor Herzl, President of the Zionist Organization wrote: "It is essential that the sufferings of Jews become worse. This will assist in realization of our plans. I have an excellent idea. I shall induce anti-Semites to liquidate Jewish wealth. Thereby, the anti-Semites will assist us in that they will strengthen the persecution and oppression of Jews. The anti-Semites shall be our best friends." 'Rot schild' (the red hexagon sign) was made the Zionist flag. 51 years later it will be adopted as flag of Israel.

In 1901, the Jews from the colonies set up in Palestine sent a delegation and told Edmond James de Rothschild: "If you wish to save the Yishuv (the Jewish settlement), first take your hands from it and for once permit the colonists to have the possibility of correcting for themselves what needs correcting." Rothschild got very angry about this and said: "I created the Yishuv, I alone. Therefore no men, neither colonists nor organizations have the right to interfere in my plans."

In 1905, a group of Rothschild-backed Zionist Jews led by Georgi Apollonovich Gapon attempted to overthrow the Tsar in Russia in a Communist Coup. They failed and were forced to flee Russia. They were given refuge in Germany.

The Jewish Encyclopedia (Vol. 2, p.497) states: "It is a somewhat curious sequel to the attempt to set up a Catholic competitor to the Rothschilds that at the present time the latter are the guardians of the papal treasure."

In 1907 Jacob Schiff, (a Rothschild), the head of Kuhn, Loeb and

Co., in a speech to the New York Chamber of Commerce, warned: "Unless we have a Central Bank with adequate control of credit resources, this country is going to undergo the most severe and far reaching money panic in its history." Suddenly America found itself in the middle of another typical run of the mill Rothschild engineered financial crisis which ruins as usual the lives of millions of innocent people throughout America and makes billions in profit for the Rothschilds.

In 1909, Jacob Schiff founded the National Association for the Advancement of the Coloured People (NAACP). This was done to incite black people into rioting, looting and other forms of disorder, in order to cause a rift between the black and white communities. Jewish historian Howard Sachar states in his book, "A History of the Jews in America": "In 1914, Professor Emeritus Joel Spingarn of Columbia University became chairman of the NAACP and recruited for its board such Jewish leaders as Jacob Schiff, Jacob Billikopf, and Rabbi Stephen Wise." Other Ashkenazi Jew co-founders included Julius Rosenthal, Lillian Wald and Rabbi Emil G. Hirsch. It was not until 1920 that the NAACP appointed its first black president, James Weldon Johnson." The president was the only black person in NAACP until recently.

On March 4, 1913, Woodrow Wilson was elected President of the United States. Shortly after his inauguration, he was visited in the White House by Ashkenazi Jew, Samuel Untermyer, of law firm 'Guggenheim, Untermyer and Marshall'. He blackmailed Wilson for the sum of $40,000 in relation to an affair Wilson had while he was a professor at Princeton University, with a fellow Professor's wife. President Wilson did not have the money, so Untermyer volunteered to pay the $40,000 out of his own pocket to the woman Wilson had had the affair with, on the condition that Wilson promise to appoint to the first vacancy on the United States Supreme Court a nominee to be recommended to President Wilson by Untermyer. Wilson agreed to this.

Jacob Schiff set up the Anti-Defamation League (ADL) in the United States, for the purpose of slandering anyone who questions or challenges the Rothschild global conspiracy as "anti-Semitic". Rothchilds set up the Federal Reserve, their last and current central bank in America. Congressman Charles Lindbergh stated following the passing of the Federal Reserve Act on December 23, 1913: "The Act establishes the most gigantic trust on earth. When the President signs this Bill, the invisible government of the monetary power will be legalized.......The greatest crime of the ages is perpetrated by this banking and currency bill." It is important to note that the Federal Reserve is a private company, it is neither Federal nor does it have any Reserve. It was conservatively estimated that profits of Fed exceed $150 billion in the first year. Federal Reserve has never once in its history published accounts.

In 1914, Rothchilds instigated the World War I. In this war, the German Rothschilds loaned money to the Germans, the British Rothschilds loaned money to the British and the French Rothschilds loaned money to the French. The Rothschilds owned the three European news agencies, Wolff (est. 1849) in Germany, Reuters (est. 1851) in England, and Havas (est. 1835) in France. The Rothschilds used Wolff to manipulate the German people into fervor for war. From around this time, the Rothschilds are rarely reported in the media, because they owned the media.

12. The Curse of Central Banks

Under the Central Banking system, the government issues a bond, and the central bank prints paper money (ordinary paper with an amount printed on it) and uses it to buy that government bond. The Government spends that money. Government pays 6% interest on the bond until it pays back the amount and redeems the bond. Thus Central bank gets 6% interest for money which it created out of thin air by printing on paper. That is a scam.

President Kennedy tried to stop this scam. He knew that it was contrary to the Constitution of the United States of America, to use Federal Reserve Bank Notes as the purported legal currency. On June 4, 1963, he signed the Executive Order 11110, which gave the Treasury Department the explicit authority: "to issue silver certificates against any silver bullion, silver, or standard silver dollars in the Treasury." The treasury printed $4 billion in $2 and $5 silver certificate bills and put into circulation, backed by silver bullion physically held there. The silver certificates and Federal Reserve currency looked alike, except one says "Federal Reserve Note" on the top while the other says "United States Note". Also, the Federal Reserve Note has a green seal and serial number while the United States Note has a red seal and serial number.

This order stripped the Rothschild Bank of its power to loan money to the United States Federal Government at interest. It challenged the "powers that exist behind U.S. and world finance – the Rothschild". The Jewish Bankers conspired with Israeli Mossad and assassinated Kennedy. His vice president Lyndon Johnson was on the pay of Jewish bankers and was in on the assassination conspiracy. He told his mistress, the night before assassination, that she need not worry about Kennedy after the next day.

President Kennedy was assassinated on November 22, 1963 in Dallas, Texas by CIA sharp shooters, who ironically were trained by Kennedy to assassinate Fidel Castro and other left-wing world leaders like Allende of Chile. All of those involved in the murder of JFK were subsequently murdered including the surgeon and medical personnel who attended him in the hospital and in the morgue. Phyllis Hall, a nurse who was part of the team that tried to save the life of JFK, later claimed he was shot by a "mystery bullet", meaning he was shot at close range by somebody either in the car or one of the CIA agents assigned to protect the president.

A patsy was arrested as the lone gunman and he was killed by a Jewish activist. Thus all trail of his assassination was closed. The senate investigation was manipulated by Jewish senators and finally a report was produced which blamed a lone gunman (patsy) with a magic bullet that took several 90 degree turns on its path and pierced Kennedy from several entry points and finally blew away his skull and disappeared. The 'lone assassin' conclusion was reached in many other assassinations ordered by bankers, before Kennedy and after Kennedy, in the history of USA.

Before the body of Kennedy became cold, Lyndon Johnson declared himself President. His first act as President was to verbally repeal the Executive Order 11110 of Kennedy and withdraw the US Treasury silver certificates (dollar bills) from circulation.

$10 and $20 US treasury bills were in printing when Kennedy was assassinated. They were never put into circulation. This Executive Order is still valid, but nobody dare to implement it for fear of the bankers. Thus, Rothschild's Federal Reserve Bank continues to create money to this day. US Treasury Notes were issued as an interest-free and debt-free currency backed by silver reserves in the U.S. Treasury.

If Executive Order 11110 was implemented, the national debt would not have reached its current level of $22.4 trillion (as of Jan-2016). All of that debt has been created since 1963. Over the years, Federal Reserve Bank drained all the gold and silver from

Fort Knox in the name of Interest. When Ronald Reagan found out that all the gold and silver was drained from Fort Knox, he tried to get treasury to print its own money and stop borrowing money from Federal Reserve Bank. Then he was shot by a lone gunman! He survived the assassination attempt and immediately withdrew his order.

Abraham Lincoln tried hard to avoid financing the civil war through the Rothschild's bank. He asked Treasury to print its own money. It was called the 'green back' because one side of the currency was printed in green color. He won the civil war without borrowing money from Rothschild's bank at 35% interest.

Rothschild, who owned 'Bank of England' and 'Bank of France' and thereby controlled the finances of both England and France, instigated the British and French to initiate, support and finance the secession of the South from the North of USA. The Czar of Russia who saw the vicious Rothschild's hand in the war, intervened by providing naval forces for the Union blockade of the South in European waters, and by letting both England and France know that if they attempted to join the Confederacy with military forces, they would also have to go to war with Russia.

Lincoln's Treasury Secretary Salmon P. Chase was a Zionist Jew. He was also an agent of Rothschild. He forced the 'National Banking Act' legislation through Congress creating a federally chartered central bank that had the power to issue U.S. Bank Notes. Lincoln could not stop that legislation, but he warned the public: "The money power preys upon the nation in time of peace and conspires against it in times of adversity. It is more despotic than monarchy, more insolent than autocracy, more selfish than bureaucracy. I see in the near future a crisis approaching that unnerves me, and causes me to tremble for the safety of our country. Corporations have been enthroned, an era of corruption will follow, and the money power of the country will endeavor to prolong its reign by working upon the prejudices of the people, until the wealth is aggregated in a few hands, and the republic is destroyed." Lincoln tried to limit the life of the bank. Then, the bankers conspired to kill him, just like the Jews conspired to Kill Jesus.

Conspirators from the Bank of Rothschild included Lincoln's Secretary of War Edwin Stanton, John Wilkes Booth, Albert Pike, Judah P. Benjamin, the Civil War campaign manager in the South for the House of Rothschild, Slidell, Admiral G.W. Baird, August Belmont (Rothschild's Northern agent) and over seventy government officials and businessmen. Booth's diary was recovered by Stanton's troops and given to investigators, but without eighteen pages. These pages, containing the conspirators' names, were later found in the attic of one of Stanton's descendants. From Booth's trunk, a coded message was found that linked him directly to Judah P. Benjamin, a Zionist Jew. The key to the code was found in Benjamin's possession.

Stanton's troops left one bridge in Washington un-guarded. The assassin, Booth, escaped by way of that bridge and went to Europe with Stanton's help. Three days later, Captain James William Boyd who resembled Booth was shot and killed as patsy. Baird and Stanton identified the body as Booth's. His body was dumped into an Arsenal Prison sinkhole used to dump dead horses. Vice - President Andrew Johnson became President and pardoned Albert Pike. Albert Pike made Andrew Johnson a thirty-third degree Mason. Vice President Andrew Johnson was on the payroll of bankers, just like Lyndon Johnson was on their payroll. When Lincoln died, his wife started screaming, "Oh, that dreadful house!" referring to Thomas W. House, a Jewish gun runner, financier, anti-Lincoln agitator and Rothschild's agent during the Civil War.

President Andrew Jackson vetoed the renewal of the charter for the Bank of the United States on July 10, 1832. In 1835, he said of the Jewish Bankers: "You are a den of vipers. I intend to rout you out, and by the Eternal God I will rout you out. If the people only understood the rank injustice of our money and banking system, there would be a revolution before morning." He referred to the bankers as 'den of vipers'. That is what Jesus called Jews of his time. The Rothschild bank sent assassins, but he escaped and then stopped his campaign against the bankers.

President, James Garfield, said: "whoever controls the supply of currency would control the business and activities of all the people." After only four months in office, President Garfield was assassinated by another lone gunman (!) sent by Rothschild bank in 1881.

Congressman Larry P. McDonald tried to expose the Rothschild's banks. He was assassinated by the Rothschild conspirators in 1983, by shooting down the plane he was traveling on. Senators John Heinz and John Tower were outspoken critics of the Federal Reserve Bank and the Eastern Establishment. They were both assassinated by Rothschild bankers in 1991, by crashing their planes. Since then, nobody has dared to ask for auditing of Federal Reserve Bank for fear of assassination by bankers.

Two other presidents were killed by poisoning because they tried to stop borrowing money from Federal Reserve Bank. When Federal Reserve Bank was made official, government also started the Federal income tax in America to pay for interest on the money borrowed by government. Now, 75% of all income tax collected by US Government is given to Federal Reserve Bank as interest on money borrowed. Now, the US Government owes 22.4 trillion dollars to Federal Reserve Bank. It is called the 'national debt'. That comes to over $58,000 for every man woman and child in America.

Many people have suggested returning to the gold standard. But that is no longer possible. Because, over 90% of all the gold in this world is hidden by Rothchilds bankers in secret bunkers. The remaining gold is not enough to support the currency of the world.

Moreover, the Zionist Satan-worshippers have already moved the world towards 'One world-Government', one world-currency and one world-army and one world-religion (Judaism for Jews, and 'noahide laws' but no religion for non-Jews). The world population will be culled through tainted vaccines that cause autism and mental and physical disorders and through diseases like AIDS and flu pandemics and through GMO foods that cause cancer and impotency and through use of poisons like sodium fluoride in drinking water. Non-Jewish population will be culled to 500 million and Jewish population will be increased to 50 million. It will be called the 'New World Order'. UN 'Agenda 21' has already been enacted by all governments allowing all these to happen. American Homeland Security has already purchased over 4.5 billion hollow point bullets used to kill people by snipers and 1.5 billion plastic coffins for mass burial of dead populations in USA. All these horrible events are planned by Satan-worshipping bankers. But this is not part of the tribulation which Christian apologists have been preaching about.

Thanks to the 'common core' based education they receive in their school, most Americans believe that Federal Reserve Bank is an agency of the United States Government. The name "Federal Reserve Bank" was designed to deceive, and it still does. Several chairmen of the FED including Greenspan, have publicly announced that FED is not owned by the government. It is privately owned. Its physical property is held under private deeds, and is subject to local taxation. Government property is not taxable. But the public still believes that FED is a government agency. It has created unimaginable wealth for Rothschilds. It controls practically everything in the lives of every human being on earth.

.
.
.
.
.
.
.

13 The Three World Wars

The secret plan of BIS to create a world currency is closely linked to the secret plan of Rothchild to create One World Government. The march towards the goal of One World Government or 'New World Order' has been steadily progressing ever since the detailed plan was hatched in 1871 by Albert Pike. Here is his plan:

---

3 World Wars

(by Albert Pike, Freemason Strategist, Zionist, in 1870.)

"*The First World War must be brought about in order to permit the Illuminati to overthrow the power of the Czars in Russia and of making that country a fortress of atheistic Communism. The divergences caused by the "agentur" (agents) of the Illuminati between the British and Germanic Empires will be used to foment this war. At the end of the war, Communism will be built and used in order to destroy the other governments and in order to weaken the religions.*

The Second World War must be fomented by taking advantage of the differences between the Fascists and the political Zionists. This war must be brought about so that Nazism is destroyed and that the political Zionism be strong enough to institute a sovereign state of Israel in Palestine. During the Second World War, International Communism must become strong enough in order to balance Christendom, which would be then restrained and held in check until the time when we would need it for the final social cataclysm."

The Third World War must be fomented by taking advantage of the differences caused by the "agentur" of the "Illuminati" between the political Zionists and the leaders of the Islamic World. The war must be conducted in such a way that Islam (the Moslem Arabic World) and political Zionism (the State of Israel) mutually destroy each other. Meanwhile the other nations, once more divided on this issue will be constrained to fight to the point of complete physical, moral, spiritual and economic exhaustion. We shall unleash the Nihilists and the atheists, and we shall provoke a formidable social cataclysm which in all its horror will show clearly to the nations the effect of absolute atheism, origin of savagery and of the most bloody turmoil. Then everywhere, the citizens, obliged to defend themselves against the world minority of revolutionaries, will exterminate those destroyers of civilization, and the multitude, disillusioned with Christianity, whose deistic spirits will from that moment be without compass or direction, anxious for an ideal, but without knowing where to render its adoration, will receive the true light through the universal manifestation of the pure doctrine of Lucifer, brought finally out in the public view. This manifestation will result from the general reactionary movement which will follow the destruction of Christianity and atheism, both conquered and exterminated at the same time." ----------- *Albert Pike*

Anyone who read history of the world can see that everything that has happened since 1870 to current date has happened as per the plan laid out by Albert Pike. Obviously, the Rothschilds are following the script.

14 Recap and Conclusion.

Minting money is not easy. Government treasury has to acquire gold and silver and copper and other metals and then melt it and measure it and mint it and store it and spend it as needed and keep accounting of all the money. Government sometimes runs out of money, especially during war preparations. Rothschild family set up RBI and promised to lend government as much money as it needs for 6% interest, if the government allows it to handle the money minting and distribution functions of the treasury. Government agreed. Every time government needs money, it will borrow from RBI for 6% interest. When government borrows money, it signs a promise to repay the amount with interest. This document or promissory note is called a treasury bond. RBI buys treasury bonds (government's promise to pay) and then pays for it with money minted by RBI. Gold and silver are heavy to carry around. So, RBI prints paper currency and mints coins with cheaper metals. RBI promises to exchange these paper currency and metal coins for gold and silver on demand.

RBI trusts the government will redeem (or pay off) the bonds it issued, with real gold and silver. Gold and silver is the only payment accepted by RBI from government. Instead of actual gold and silver, RBI has a treasury bond (promissory note from government) sitting in its vaults. Instead of gold and silver coins, RBI issues paper currency with a promise to exchange it for gold and silver on demand. So, RBI money is also a promissory note like the Treasury bond. People trust the RBI currency because they believe that RBI has enough gold and silver (or at least government bonds) sitting in its vaults as reserve. This is called the <u>reserve banking</u> system. Nobody has ever asked to see how much reserve (gold and silver) is sitting on the shelves of RBI. Those who demand to see it (audit the central bank) mysteriously ends up dead.

Rothschild family has become enormously wealthy over the years through criminal activities and various scams and frauds. They and their banks are dishonest and fraudulent. Since nobody audits it, RBI can print 15 times as much money as it has in its vaults (reserve). Printing more money than the reserve is called <u>fractional reserve</u> banking. All the money they create is lent to either government or to other banks at 6% interest. The money that circulates in the society will lose its value by 6% every year. In about 15 years, RBI will earn as much money in interest as the principal.

To put in figures:
Government gives an interest bearing bond (promissory note) for Rs.100 to RBI.
RBI prints Rs.100 on paper and gives to Government.
Every year, Government will pay Rs. 6 (6%) to RBI as interest on the bonds.
RBI prints Rs.1400 more, using the bond of Rs.100 as fractional reserve, and lend it to other banks at agreed upon rate of, let us say, 6%.
RBI will earn Rs.90 in interest every year.

That is tremendous amount of profit without any real investment. Also, the govt. is in debt to RBI for Rs. 100. Other banks are in debt to RBI for Rs. 1400.
After one year, total amount of currency printed = Rs.1500.
Total amount needed to pay off all the debt= 1500 + 90=Rs.1590 (which is Rs.90 more than all the money printed).
That means the government and the banks have to continue to be in debt. This is a perpetual debt because all the money in circulation in the whole country is less than the amount that is owed to RBI. Therefore, there is no way to pay back all the debt.

Lender can dictate the terms to the debtor. Thus, RBI is able to dictate to Government how to govern the country. RBI will naturally order Govt. to collect all the gold and silver from its citizens and use that to pay interest to RBI. So, the government had to set up a rigorous tax collection program (revenue service). Citizens are not likely to part with their treasures easily. So, a police force has to be created to enforce the tax collection programs. Thus, creation of a central bank (RBI) brings with it creation of revenue collection service and police force to enforce the collection.

If the citizens do not pay, their property may be confiscated and they may be put in jail and they may even be killed. Government's ability to collect taxes is only as good as it ability to inflict heavy pain and destruction and death upon the citizens. RBI's ability to collect money from government is only as good as its ability to inflict pain on the government and citizens. How can a private corporation inflict pain on sovereign government?

RBI's owners (Rothschilds) have very powerful collection agents and collection techniques. If the government refuses to pay, Rothschild may send its agents to foment civil war within the country and overthrow the government, kill the government leaders, and form a new government with his owns agents. Rothschild may even order an external war against the country. America and NATO countries take orders from Rothschilds. These countries may be ordered to attack the non-paying country under spurious pretexts like bringing democracy to the country or ridding the country of non-existent 'weapons of mass destruction' (WMD). After suffering enormous destruction, death and loss of territory, the government will gladly agree to pay.

Bank (promissory) notes printed by RBI are the only official currency of the country. RBI notes are paper and it has no intrinsic value. Therefore bank notes cannot be bought or sold as a commodity. RBI owns all its notes and it can only be borrowed on interest by government and other banks.

Banks which borrow from RBI, practice fractional reserve banking. Let us assume that Banks borrow at 6% interest. They may keep that borrowed money as fractional reserve and then lend out up to 15 times the reserve amount to customers at higher interest rate.

Let us assume the customer interest rate is 10%. The difference between the interest banks pay to RBI and the interest they collect from customers is Bank's profit.
For example:
Bank borrows Rs.100 from RBI at 6% interest.
Based on that Rs.100 as fractional reserve, it lends out Rs.1500 at, say 10%, interest.
In one year, bank receives Rs. 1500 + 150 = 1650.
Bank pays Rs.100+6=106 to RBI.
The Bank's Gross profit = 1650-106 = 1544.
Let us assume the cost of doing business (rent, utility, salary, etc.) = Rs. 500.
Bank's net profit = Rs.1544 – 500 = Rs. 1044.

Thus, money multiplies at several levels. Money supply increases rapidly. More money can buy more goods and services. If goods and services increase corresponding to the growth of money supply, prosperity will increase. If available goods and services do not increase, more money will chase fewer goods and services. That will lead to price inflation. Price inflation means reduction of currency's buying power. Price inflation will erode People's savings. As time go by, higher and higher percentage of the gross domestic production (GDP) of the country will be needed to service the debt. Eventually, all of GDP may be required for servicing the debt. Thus, in Zimbabwe, in 2015, 35trillion Zimbabwe dollar was needed to buy US $1. In 21st century, thousands starve to death in Brazil which produce abundant food crops because most of the food production is exported to pay interest on its debt.

Every country that has a central bank and debt (interest) based currency will follow the same path and reach the same situation. Only a violent social revolution or external war, both of which will bring about death and destruction, can reset the currency and restore order. When and how these things will happen depends on the policies of central bank. Each social revolution and war will bring the country closer to be part of 'One-World-Government-under-Rothschild' (New World Order).

Enslaving a whole sovereign nation and keeping it enslaved is an enormous task. Only ruthless, violent force can keep a nation enslaved. It took a large army of British soldiers with guns and cannons to enslave India and keep it enslaved. India was a bunch of small primitive sword-wielding kingdoms which fought each other. As people got educated, resistance to enslavement increased and the British had to flee India. Over centuries, Rothschilds have learned the historic lessons well and they have spun intricate spider nets to keep the nations trapped within their control, in their march towards NWO.

Rothschilds have created International Bank of Settlements, International Monetary Fund, World Bank, and Federal Reserve Bank. These institutions constitute the first ring in Rothschild's monetary death trap. In modern interconnected world, no country can survive long without international trade. International trade is practically impossible without converting the payer-nation's currency into recipient-nation's currency. Only IBS can provide that conversion. IBS will do business with only Rothschild-owned central banks. Cuba, North Korea, Iran, Afghanistan, Syria and Libya had no Rothschild-owned central banks. They had to resort to barter agreements to do their limited international trade. IMF and WB also work exclusively with countries that have Rothschild–owned central banks.

These nations however did not succumb to the boycott by IBS, IMF and WB. They also survived various attempts by bankers to create civil wars, assassination of the leaders, etc. But they could not escape Rothschild's next step – war. Rothschilds originated and controls UN, according to the roadmap to NWO laid out by Albert Pyke in 1871. Rothschild unleashed the power of UN resolutions against these countries. Then, on behest of bankers, the military of USA and NATO attacked these countries in the guise of enforcing

UN resolutions. After destroying Iraq, Afghanistan and Libya, and killing their leaders and most of their people, new puppet regimes and Rothschild-owned central banks were installed. These puppet governments now rule the population for the benefit of Rothschild and American corporations. Now, Syria, Cuba, Iran and North Korea are the only countries left without a Rothschild-owned central bank.

Rothschild's ultimate goal is to establish NWO according to the plan laid out by Albert Pyke in 1871. People have come to accept inflation as a natural phenomenon. But that is not true. In Soviet Union they were able to keep the inflation at 0% for more than 75 years. The price of a loaf of bread, and a phone call and a ride on the underground railway, for example, stayed constant at 1 penny. Countries that did not have Rothschild-owned central banks had 0% inflation as long as there were no major external wars. <u>Inflation is caused by the interest-based banking system.</u>

Even though Central banks are the most powerful weapon to enslave a nation, there are other forces at work. Public opinion, education and information matters. So, Rothschilds bought up all news reporting agencies and all the mainstream and alternative media outlets including TV, Radio, Newspapers, book publishing, internet and social media like Facebook and twitter. All the information one receives, from the time of birth to time of death is Rothschild-controlled propaganda. School and Universities teach Rothschild-controlled propaganda. Economists holding PhDs from respected Universities believe Federal Reserve Bank is owned by US government. Even Nobel laureates believe inflation is a natural phenomenon like gravity. Theory of evolution is another major falsehood taught by Universities everywhere. Bankers create and control all sides of political philosophies. Thus, in USA bankers own the Democratic Party and the Republican Party and even the third parties. That is why the policies and behavior of the governments remain the same no matter who gets elected. Rothschild ordered creation of Communism, Nietzscheism, Fascism, Nihilism and

Nazism. This was all in accordance with the road map to NWO laid out by Albert Pyke in 1871. Fascism and Nazism were used by Rothschild to bring about WWII.

What does the future hold?

According to the IMF reports, worldwide debt owed to bankers is more than 200% of the world GDP. That means bankers can impose their conditionalities on nations of the world. In the name of saving the world financial system, bankers may impose a 'world-currency' (SDRs of IMF, perhaps) upon the nations. That will bring the world closer to one world government and NWO under Rothschild. Somewhere between all this, a world-wide reduction in population (culling) will take place. In the NWO there will be only 500 million people, as prescribed in the Georgia Guide Stones.

------ *END* ------

OTHER BOOKS BY SAME AUTHOR

Holy Bible: Genesis (Study Bible)
Holy Bible: Exodus, (Study Bible)
Holy Bible: Leviticus, (Study Bible)
Holy Bible: Numbers, (Study Bible)
Holy Bible: Deuteronomy (Study Bible)

Gospel Of Mathew – (Study Bible)
Gospel Of Mark – (Study Bible)
Gospel Of Luke – (Study Bible)
Gospel Of John – (Study Bible)
The Revelation (Study Bible)
Holy Cow! What Did Mark write?

Was Jesus Black?
Jesus : The Eastern Star
Conversion of Terrorist
Origin of Everything - The Creationist Version
My Journey from Islam to Christianity
Pedophile Priest
Search for Mr. Almighty
Song of the Blind Girl (Movie)
Lucy's Law   (Movie)
Trial Of A Monster (Movie)
The President Goes to Heaven   (Movie)
Who Killed Aliyah ?   (Movie)
Big Black Little Blonde
A Returning Veteran
Secret Codes
Fukushima Report
Figure Skater
Reserve Bank of India
.
.
.
.

ABOUT THE AUTHOR

The Author has spent several years researching the Ancient Scriptures, Ancient History and Times and Practices of Ancient Civilizations and visiting locations and talking to experts and locals and those in the know. You may contact author by e-mail at:
cindynet.marktom@yandex.ru

ACKNOWLEDGMENTS

The Author is obligated to many people for their contributions to the making of this book. It is difficult to thank them all by name.
Special thanks to the researchers and analysts and linguists and ancient manuscript keepers,
'The Bodleian Libraries of the University of Oxford',
'The Biblioteca Apostolica Vaticana (BAV)',
'The Library of Congress',
'The Lenin State Library of Moscow',
'The Admont Benedictine Monastery in Austria',
'The British Library'

LEGAL DISCLAIMERS

This book is entirely a work of fiction. The names, characters and incidents portrayed are the work of the author's imagination. Any resemblance to actual persons, events or localities, living or dead, is entirely coincidental. Any resemblance between the characters, places and events, depicted in this work of fiction and real people, places, events, either living or dead, is unintentional and purely coincidental. This is a work of fiction. All the characters and events portrayed in this book are either products of the author's imagination or are used factiously. Events described in this book should not be taken as factual.

www.ingramcontent.com/pod-product-compliance
Lightning Source LLC
Chambersburg PA
CBHW060355190526
45169CB00002B/605